INSIGHT COMPACT GUIDES

SC

Compact Guide: Scotland is the ultimate quick-reference guide to this beautiful country. It tells you all you need to know about Scotland's attractions, from the rural delights of the lowlands to the rugged splendour of the Highlands and islands, from the romance of its castles and glens to the vibrant culture of its cities.

This is just one title in *Apa Publications'* new series of pocket-sized, easy-to-use guidebooks intended for the independent-minded traveller. *Compact Guides* pride themselves on being up-to-date and authoritative. They are in essence mini travel encyclopedias, designed to be comprehensive yet portable, as well as readable and reliable.

Star Attractions

An instant reference to some of Scotland's most popular tourist attractions to help you on your way.

Edinburgh Castle p14

High Kirk of St Giles p18

Glasgow p21

Dumfries p37

Glamis p46

Dunnottar Castle p 47

Hebrides p 61

Oban p 69

Edinburgh Castle Guard p14

Glencoe p74

Distillery, p75

SCOTLAND

Introduction

Places

Culture

Leisure

Practical Information

Scotland – Land of Surprises

Opposite: George Square in Glasgow

For many people Scotland is a target for jokes about haggis, stinginess and men in skirts – the country of bagpipes and whisky. Those of a less frivolous nature may associate it with beautiful, rugged scenery and the oil rigs off the North Sea coast.

Like most caricatures and generalisations, these are based on fact, but are only a small part of the picture. Some American visitors will not see a single kilted Scotsman playing the bagpipes during the whole of their Scottish holiday, only to encounter one at a function back home organised by people who have family ties with a Scottish clan. Jokes about the legendary stinginess of the Scots are so widespread that they are even exploited by the Bank of Scotland to advertise its services. But within Great Britain the Scots are known for quite different things: for example the most unhealthy diet and (as a direct consequence) the highest rate of heart disease in the European Union. But they are also famed for the rejection of the ruling Conservative Party by a large majority of the population, for a crime rate much lower than England's, and for an anarchic sense of humour.

The Scots increasingly try to sharpen the distinction between their country and England and to emphasise their own identity. Nothing annoys them more than the classification of the cultural achievements of their ancestors as 'English literature' or 'English architecture' – two areas, incidentally, where there is no lack of famous Scottish names. When the Englishman Henry Havelock Ellis compiled a list of 'British geniuses' in 1904, he established that from a statistical point of view the Scots were far too highly represented.

Thus we have a country which on one hand has its share of social and political problems, of which continental Europe is more or less unaware, and on the other conjures up a number of stock images. The surprising thing about all this is that Scotland nevertheless fulfils almost all expectations: the visitor who wants bagpipe music, kilts and whisky distilleries will find them at the Highland Games and on the 'Malt Whisky Trail' in Speyside. The lover of solitude, grandiose landscapes and relatively unspoilt nature will be equally rewarded, and those in pursuit of the cultural delights of art, architecture and the performing arts will have time for little else.

View towards Ben More

Shades of past glories, Glamis

Position and size

Scotland occupies the northern third of mainland Great Britain together with the surrounding islands (the Hebrides and the Orkney and Shetland Islands). Edinburgh is at approximately the same latitude as Copenhagen and

Moscow, while the northernmost tip of the Scottish mainland is level with Stockholm.

The country has a surface area of 30,394 sq miles (788,722 sq km), 34 percent of the area of Great Britain. It is divided into three geological regions: the Southern Uplands is a 50-mile (80-km) band of hills with a maximum height of just over 2,625ft (800 metres) which extends from the English border to just south of Edinburgh and Glasgow. These two cities lie in the central area known as the Lowlands, a strip of relatively flat country running from the southwest to the northeast and the most fertile and densely populated part of Scotland. In the north it borders on the Highlands, which are in turn divided by the fault known as the Great Glen (Loch Ness, Loch Lochy and Loch Linnhe): on one side are the Eastern Highlands with the Grampian Mountains, while the area to the west and north of the Great Glen is the most thinly populated part of Great Britain, with mountains up to 4,265ft (1,300 metres) in height, sparse vegetation and the oldest geological formations in Western Europe.

A friendly native

Nesting gulls

Landscape and wildlife

With the exception of a few inaccessible strips of coast and remote, uninhabited islands, even the wildest and most sparsely populated parts of Scotland cannot really be classified as completely unspoilt. Forestry, sheep breeding and management of the land for hunting purposes have affected the flora and fauna even in those areas far from population centres and main roads, and the most attractive areas are now increasingly at risk due to the expansion of tourism.

The suitability of the Lowlands and Southern Uplands for farming was recognized by the early settlers and exploited correspondingly, but until the late-18th and early 19th century subsistence farming was the rule in the Highlands, and this interfered relatively little with the natural landscape – although the population's need for wood destroyed the old Caledonian (north Scottish) forests.

In Scotland you are never very far from the sea, and the rocky coastline ranks with the ranges of almost treeless hills and mountains as the most typical natural features of Scotland. It is no wonder that some of the largest and most varied colonies of sea birds in Europe are to be found on the islands and coasts in the north and west. In addition, in certain areas attempts are being made to prevent the extinction of local species such as wild cats, otters and ospreys, which have already dwindled greatly in numbers.

Climate

The Scottish climate is characterised by mild Atlantic weather in the west (through the influence of the Gulf

Stream), with high rainfall and relatively small variations in temperature – in winter it is less cold, but in summer less warm than the eastern North Sea Coast, where conditions are harsher but it rains far less frequently. The Edinburgh area, where it rains on average 175 days a year, has the lowest rainfall, and the Outer Hebrides the highest (around 250 days a year).

Rapid changes in the weather must always be reckoned with in Scotland – stout shoes and an anorak are advisable for anyone intending to spend more than ten minutes in the open air, even in summer. But 'rapid change' must not automatically be interpreted as a change for the worse.

The weather can change dramatically

The best time to visit Scotland is between the middle of June and the first weeks of September, when daytime temperatures are often over 68°F (20°C). Mid-May to mid-June and the end of September/beginning of October are quieter because they do not coincide with the British school holidays, and there are also unlikely to be severe storms – in the northwest early autumn is often the pleasantest time of year. The relatively short winter sports season is at its height in January and February.

Population and religion

Scotland has a population of 5.1 million, of Celtic, Anglo-Saxon and Scandinavian origin. However, in the late-20th century, even on the remote Orkney Islands a substantial number of the 'local' people do not even speak with a Scottish accent, let alone belong to a family that has been associated with the country for generations. Communities with such families do still exist, especially in the Outer Hebrides where a few thousand people continue to speak Gaelic, but in general immigration and exchanges of population with other parts of Great Britain have made Scotland as cosmopolitan as other European regions. Some experts nevertheless consider that one reason why the Highlands have the highest suicide rate in Britain is the breakdown of traditional social structures.

Waiting their turn at the Highland Gathering

The Presbyterian Church, the Church of Scotland, is generally regarded as the embodiment of Scotland's national characteristics: its Calvinistic ethos places a high value on hard work and obedience to authority, but also on intellectual independence. Love of argument, pursued to the point of stubbornness, is said to be a particular characteristic of the smaller Protestant groups known as the Free Churches.

Stained glass in St Giles Cathedral

The existence of a state church may give the erroneous impression that Scotland is a purely Protestant country, but in 1987/88 almost as many Scots were adherents of the Roman Catholic faith (794,000) as of the Church of Scotland (823,000). There is a particularly high proportion of Catholics in industrial towns such as Glasgow and Dundee, which have large Irish populations, and there are also old-established Catholic communities in the Highlands and the southern islands of the Outer Hebrides.

St Andrew's Cross

Government and politics

Geographically, Scotland could be termed the northernmost province of Great Britain, but this is a description guaranteed to provoke the wrath of most of its population. The nature of the British monarchy and the absence of a written constitution have resulted in a number of contradictions: Scotland thus has its own legal system, which differs considerably from the English one, but has no representative body (in the form of a local parliament or similar institution), so all the laws are passed in London. Adapting them to the Scottish legal system is the responsibility of the Secretary of State for Scotland, who is a member of the cabinet of the British government.

This form of administration has done nothing to gain support in Scotland for the Conservative Party, which rules from London and clings resolutely to the status quo. The other parties in parliament are arguing the case for regional autonomy: Labour, by far the strongest party in Scotland, and the Liberal Democrats are supporting various federal models for the UK. The Scottish National Party, in its own words averse to any form of 'ethnic nationalism' wants 'an independent Scotland which is part of the European Union'. The 'Nats', as they are known, only obtained 32% of the votes in the European elections in 1994.

SNP Headquarters with door detail

One example of the political contradictions is the privatisation of the Central Scotland Water Development Board which is proceeding apace in defiance of public opinion – a comprehensive referendum in the Strathclyde region revealed that 98 percent of participants were against it. The regional administrative reform, introduced only in 1975, which created 12 regions and districts subordinate to them, is being rejected again by London.

A Highland fling

Economy and environment

The Scottish economy is dependent for its survival on two industries: tourism and North Sea oil. Tourism and the related industries (crafts, etc.) provide work for far more people than any other branch of the Scottish economy, while oil produces enormous tax revenues, and large profits for successful businesses, but neither are without their problems. Areas attractive to tourists are in danger of being spoiled by so many visitors, and work in the service industries is often badly paid and carried out by unqualified people. Drilling for oil (and gas) off the North Sea coast is a crisis-prone undertaking, most of the tax goes straight to London and only a few of the successful enterprises are in Scottish hands.

Ferry at Port Glasgow

The heavy industry for which Scotland was once famous has almost completely disappeared – in the past five years the last but one of the large shipyards, the last steelworks and the last large colliery in Scotland have closed down. Hopes for the industrial sector are now pinned on the development of high-tech firms. The 1980s were supposed to mark the establishment of a 'Silicon Glen' between Edinburgh and Glasgow, but even here the first crisis has already resulted in considerable losses. While Scotland is hoping to make a breakthrough on the international market in the fields of biotechnology and genetics, more solid, if more modest prospects are provided by export-oriented trades and industries, some of which already have a long tradition in Scotland: food processing (cakes, jams, etc.), textiles (knitwear, tweed), whisky and fish-farming (in particular salmon).

The conflict between conserving the environment and providing jobs is particularly acute in the poorest parts of Scotland. For example, there is a plan to start 'super quarries' in the midst of the most beautiful landscape on the west coast (Glensanda, north of Oban) and on the Hebridean island of Harris (Lingerbay and Maraig). Mountains will be levelled to provide metal for road-building. If the plans go ahead, by the end of the century there will be six quarries in operation with an annual turnover of £360 million, 1,200 employees and an expected total yield of around eighteen thousand million tons of stone – which would irrevocably change the scenery and ecological balance of the areas concerned. As always with such issues, there is a division of opinion amongst the local people: some of them welcome the prospect of a regular source of income without having to leave their home region, while others not only deplore the damage to the environment, but see the plans as a threat to their livelihood from the tourist trade, livestock or fishing.

Waiting for the big one

Historical Highlights

c 6000BC Findings of mussel shells and stone tools indicate that there were hunters and gatherers living on the Scottish coasts at this time.

c 4000BC The first signs of settlement (houses built on stilts). Burial cairns and standing stones are typical of the transition from the Stone Age to the Bronze Age. Numerous finds in the Orkneys and Hebrides indicate that the islands in the north and west were heavily populated in the Stone and Bronze Ages.

800BC The first immigration of Celtic tribes from Gallia to the British Isles. The tribe later given the name of Picts (the painted ones) by the Romans settles in the far north.

c AD82 onwards The Roman Emperor Vespasian dispatches troops to the north to subjugate the Picts; in the area north of Dundee (Mons Graupius) the legions of Gnaeus Julius Agricola defeat an army of Picts led by Calgacus, whom Tacitus credits with saying of the Romans that 'They create barren wastes and call it peace'. The Picts withdraw to the Highlands and develop effective guerilla tactics. All attempts to bring peace to the region fail, including the final endeavour by Emperor Septimus Severus in the year 208. The Romans resort to building fortifications along the border (Hadrian's Wall.)

c 3rd century the Celtic Scots (from whom the name Scotland is derived), emigrate to Scotland from Ireland, introducing the Gaelic language and the clan system. The first Christian missionaries venture into the country from the south, but the Celtic religion, based on natural phenomena, remains dominant.

563 The systematic conversion of Scotland to Christianity begins with the arrival of the Irish monk Columba, who establishes a community of monks on Iona.

c 800 Normans, Danes and Varangians invade Scotland (in 795 the monastery of Iona is attacked). After the first wave of Viking sea raids, Norwegian jarls begin to settle in the north and gradually become assimilated: the Viking prince Thorfinn, ruler of large parts of the northwestern mainland as well as the Orkney and Shetland Islands c 1050, grew up at the court of the Scottish King Malcolm II.

843 The Scottish Prince Kenneth MacAlpin forms an alliance with the Picts against the Vikings and becomes the first Scottish king.

1165 When William the Lion ascends the Scottish throne, his kingdom encompasses almost the whole of Scotland as it is today. English is the main language spoken at court and the society is organized according to the Franco-Norman feudal system.

After 1200 A long period of dispute over succession. The English King Edward I tries to exploit the situation, but is countered by two opponents who become Scottish heroes: William Wallace defeats Edward in 1297 in the battle of Stirling Bridge, but in the following year the Scots are beaten at Falkirk. In 1306 Robert Bruce is crowned King of Scotland but is forced to flee from Edward. After Edward's death Bruce returns to power and defeats the English in 1314 at the Battle of Bannockburn. With the coronation of Bruce's grandson Robert the Steward in 1371, dynastic stability is re-established. The royal house, later bearing the name of Stuart, rules continuously until early in the 17th century.

1350–62 Scotland is ravaged twice by the Black Death. It is almost fifty years before the country recovers from the resulting depopulation and economic decline.

15th century Founding of the first universities in Scotland – St Andrews, Glasgow (1451) and Aberdeen (1495).

1520 onwards The first Lutheran tracts are brought into the country by merchants. The Catholic Church is put under increasing pressure, especially when Henry VIII of England, who broke with Rome in 1534, trys to force the betrothal of his son Edward to Mary Stuart, a child of two ('The Rough Wooing'). The Scottish royal family turns to France for support, but the population reacts negatively to the presence of French troops. Spokesman of the resistance is the Calvinist John Knox, who stirs up considerable public feeling against 'papism'.

1560 The 'Reformation Parliament' officially abolishes the Catholic state church.

1561 Mary Stuart ascends the throne, but is obliged to abdicate in 1567 in favour of her one-year-old son, James VI.

1603 James VI becomes James I of England, and with the personal Union of the Crowns the Stuarts rule Scotland and England for over a hundred years – interrupted in 1649–60 by the English civil war and the rule of Oliver Cromwell.

1707 After influential members of the Scottish Parliament and the Church have been persuaded with gifts of money and privileges, the 'Articles of Union', the Union of the Parliaments of England and Scotland, are ratified: the United Kingdom of Great Britain comes into being.

1714–19 When the British throne passes to George I of Hanover in 1714, followers of the House of Stuart try to establish the claims of the son of James VII/II to the throne. The first uprising, mainly involving Highland clans under the leadership of the Earl of Mar, fails when the Duke of Argyll in the Lowlands, loyal to the crown, sends an army to fight the rebels. The second attempt in 1719 is crushed at the outset.

1745–6 With help from France the third Jacobite uprising, this time led by 'Bonnie Prince Charlie', the grandson of the last James, is initially successful. However it soon becomes apparent that the Stuart Prince cannot rely on the support of the rich Lowlands, and the decisive battle of Culloden ends in a crushing defeat for the Jacobites.

---

c 1750 onwards With the advent of the industrial revolution Scotland's economy grows apace (steam engines, the textile and iron industries, shipbuilding, coal mining, overseas trade). The 'Scottish Enlightenment' produces not only great artists but also brilliant engineers and philosophers (e.g. James Watt, Thomas Telford, David Hume, Adam Smith). The Highland clans, tartans and bagpipes are invested with a new romantic aura, but at the same time people are being evicted forcibly from extensive areas of the northwest (the 'Highland clearances').

1820 As the increasing rationalisation of the textile industry puts weavers out of work, there are riots by the workers ('The Radical Wars') which are brutally suppressed; it is not until 1877, with the introduction of the Factory Acts, that working hours and conditions in industry are regulated by law.

After 1945 Scotland's war industries switch to the production of consumer goods. With the post-war economic boom, regional issues throughout Great Britain take a back seat.

1975 The commercial exploitation of North Sea oil is commenced off the east coast of Scotland.

1979 Partial political autonomy is rejected as a result of a referendum. Although the majority of participating voters favoured such autonomy, the turnout was only 63 percent, and the central Labour government had ruled that 40 percent of all those entitled to vote had to be in favour. Subsequently, 11 members of the Scottish National Party (SNP) join a vote of censure against the government – which falls by one vote. In the ensuing general election, Margaret Thatcher is voted into power and promptly makes it clear that any form of home rule is out of the question.

1994 In the European elections the SNP poles only 32 percent of the Scottish vote, confirming its steady decline as a political force. The Conservative government continues to rule out any prospect of devolution.

The Highland Clearances

The clearance of vast tracts of northwest Scotland between 1784 and 1850 is one of the saddest chapters in the history of the Highlands. After the defeat of the third Jacobite uprising in 1746, the lands of many clan chiefs were confiscated. By the time they were restored by the government in 1784, many chiefs were living in Edinburgh or London and employed administrators to obtain maximum profits on their behalf. Sheep farming, which produced the highest returns, was introduced to the area on a massive scale. Lowland herders moved in and existing tenants were forcibly driven from their homes. Many had to leave Scotland altogether.

By the time of the last clearances in 1853–4 the Highlands of Wester Ross and Sutherland had been almost completely depopulated. The damage caused can still be seen today in the overgrown remains of villages dotting the region.

Edinburgh Castle
Preceding pages: Eilean Donan Castle

Guarding the nation's treasures

Looking the part

Route 1

★★★ Edinburgh

After London, Edinburgh attracts more visitors than any other city in Great Britain. The castle is the most frequently visited British tourist attraction outside London. As these two statistics indicate, Edinburgh is the alternative British metropolis, countering the overwhelming political and cultural influence of London. The city is also equipped to accommodate far more guests than its size would seem to merit: during the internationally famous festival in August the streets of the inner city are packed with people, and all available beds are reserved months in advance.

While this may make Edinburgh sound rather daunting, nothing could be further from the truth. One of the most architecturally uniform (and beautiful) cities in Europe, it is a welcoming place where visitors spend as much time as possible soaking up the atmosphere and enjoying the many sights. The 18th-century town planners divided the town neatly into the primarily neoclassical New Town and the Old Town with its narrow winding streets. The Castle, perched on top of its precipitous hill above the city gives Edinburgh its unmistakable skyline.

History

The hill, called Castle Rock, is known to have been settled since the Bronze Age. When it was taken by the Angles in 638BC, King Edwin chose it for the site of his castle. One suggested origin of the name Edinburgh is that it is a derivation of 'Edwin's Burgh'.

The capital of Scotland was transferred here from Dunfermline by King David I, and with the founding of the Abbey of Holyrood in 1128 the town grew along the axis between the Castle and the monastery that is today known as the Royal Mile.

Edinburgh rose to prosperity in the second half of the 15th century: the first city wall, built in 1450, had to be replaced in 1513 by a second boundary, due to the town's expansion. In 1561 Edinburgh became the seat of Mary Stuart's government and her successors continued to rule from here until 1603, when her son James VI of Scotland became James I of England as a result of the Union of the Crowns, and moved his residence and hence the centre of power to London.

In the latter half of the 18th century Edinburgh's second period of prosperity began with flurry of building activity – in 1767, in order to ease the pressure on the cramped Old Town, the architect James Craig was commissioned to design the New Town north of the castle. The generously proportioned district has been carefully preserved in its original form. When King George IV paid a ceremonial visit to Edinburgh in 1822, the first monarch to do so for over a hundred years, he acknowledged the importance of the city as the historic centre of the 'Scottish Enlightenment', domain of the intellectual elite and seat of the judiciary and administration.

Local insignia

Sights

★★ **Edinburgh Castle** ❶ with its bird's-eye view of the surrounding streets is a good place to get your bearings before setting out on a walk through the city. The impressive complex itself also has much to offer. Within its walls is the oldest building in the city, St Margaret's Chapel, built between 1070 and 1090, and the apartments of Mary Stuart and other sections of the complex are also open to the public. In the Crown Room are the Honours of Scotland: the sceptre, crown and sword dating from the 15th–16th centuries symbolise the independence of Scotland, which is why a clause was added to the Act of Union of 1707, when the parliaments of England and Scotland were united, to the effect that the insignia could never be removed from Scotland.

In the castle courtyard

The inner courtyard is surrounded by buildings in a variety of styles, evidence that throughout the centuries buildings were constantly being added, pulled down and altered. A rebuilding project is in progress at the moment that will continue until 1997 and may involve the temporary closure of parts of the castle.

The hammerbeam roof of the Great Hall

The forecourt, the Castle Esplanade, is the setting of the **Edinburgh Military Tattoo**, held every summer, when the Scottish regiments parade in full regalia to the music of the bagpipes. Within the castle complex, British military history is commemorated with the Scottish National War Memorial and the United Services Museum.

Royal Mile shops and pub

Only a few paces from the entrance to the castle is the **Scotch Whisky Heritage Centre,** where, riding in a kind of hollowed-out whisky vat, visitors are guided through the history of the Scottish national drink.

From the steep approach to the castle there is a good view over the ★ **Royal Mile** (divided into Castlehill, Lawnmarket, High Street and Canongate). From here to Holyroodhouse it is almost exactly a mile (1½km) – although it may seem much longer: there are so many interesting things to see that not everyone gets to the end.

Castlehill ❷ has numerous unusual buildings. Below the Whisky Centre is Cannonball House – with a cannon ball embedded in the west gable, said to have been fired from the Castle during one of the many sieges. At the beginning of Ramsay Lane is Ramsay Gardens, a residential house dating from 1894, built by the eccentric

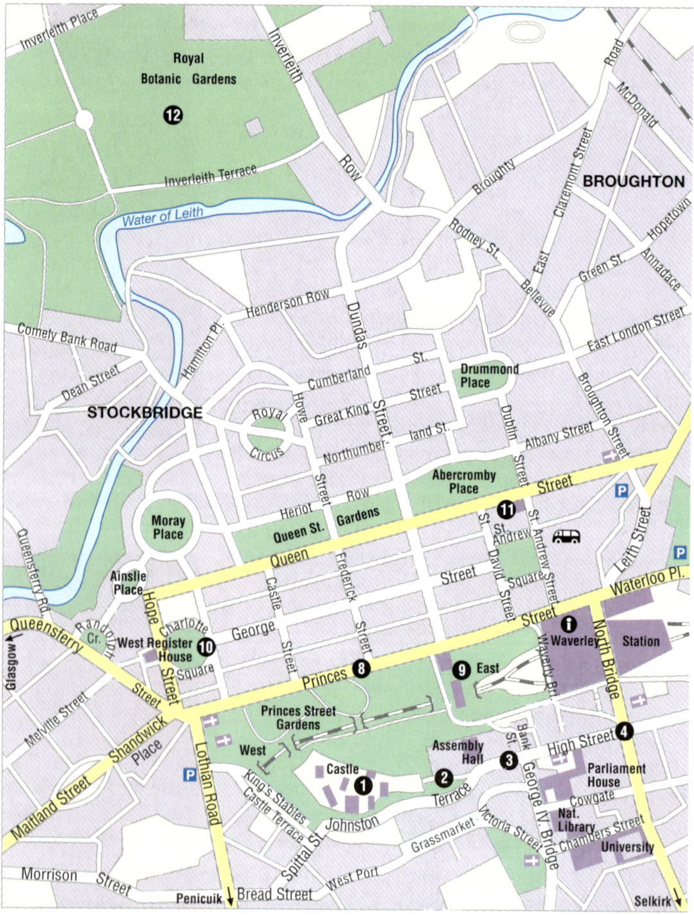

Patrick Geddes and marking the start of the much-needed Old Town renovation – by the end of the 19th century the quarter had completely degenerated. On the corner opposite is the Outlook Tower with the **Camera Obscura** on the roof. The building dates from the 17th century and the first Camera Obscura was installed in 1853. With the superior instrument in operation today it is still a fascinating experience – for example, it's the only way the neo-Gothic stonemasonry 230ft (70m) up on the Tolbooth Church can be admired close up.

Where Castlehill joins the **Lawnmarket** ❸ is the first of the small side streets, enclosed courtyards and cul-de-sacs typical of the Old Town: Milne's Court and James Court. When the present complex was built in 1700, it was one of the most desirable addresses in Edinburgh. One building between James Court and Lawnmarket, however,

The genuine article

James Court

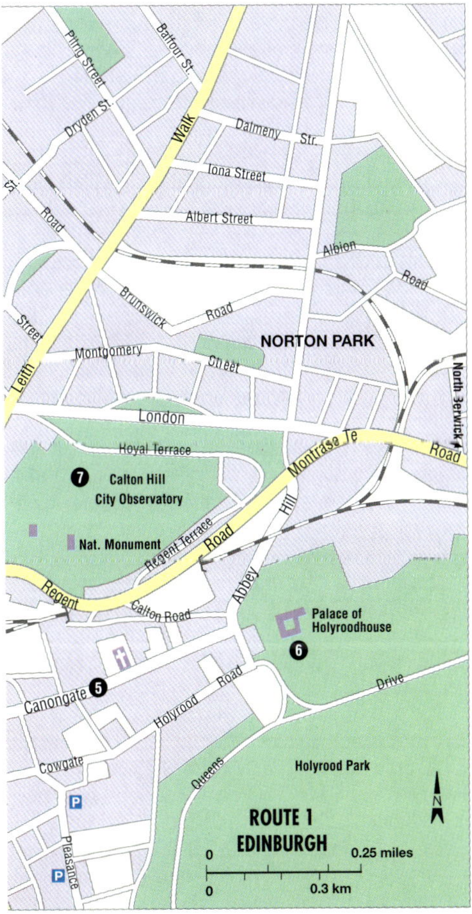

Robert Burns

High Kirk of St Giles

John Knox and his house

is a hundred years older: **Gladstone's Land** ('land' in Scots dialect is a house for several families) has been restored as an elegant 17th-century town house and is open to the public. Next door in Lady Stair's Close, **Lady Stair's House**, from the same period, houses a museum full of memorabilia relating to Robert Burns, Walter Scott and Robert Louis Stevenson.

There is a connection between Stevenson and Brodie's Close opposite: it is named after Deacon Brodie, hanged in 1788, who was a highly respected town councillor by day and a burglar by night, and is said to have been the inspiration for Stevenson's novel *Dr Jekyll and Mr Hyde*.

From the Lawnmarket the impressive ★ **High Kirk of St Giles** with its crowned tower is visible jutting out into the **High Street** ❹. The exterior – with the exception of the tower – dates from the 19th century, and only the interior gives an idea of how far back the building really goes; the oldest parts of it date from the 14th century, when it was built on the site of an even earlier, Norman church. St Giles stands on the only piece of flat ground between the Castle and Holyroodhouse: Parliament Square. The inside of Parliament House on the south side of the square, in particular the Great Hall, is also worth seeing.

On the other side of the major junction with the main road, North Bridge/South Bridge, is the Scandic Crown Hotel, a modern concrete building with a facade designed to blend in with the surrounding houses. Diagonally opposite in Chalmer's Close is Trinity College Church, which is built with old materials, but is no more 'genuine' than the Scandic Crown. The original 15th-century building which stood down in the valley was demolished in 1848 to make way for railway lines, and 25 years later rebuilt (although never fully completed) at its present location. Close by is a 16th-century house which, although it looks as unreal as a film set, has in fact changed hardly at all in the course of its history. **John Knox's House** is today a museum dedicated to the memory of the reformer and preacher who is said to have lived there (although all that is certain is that it belonged to a man by the not uncommon name of Knox). Take either of the streets opposite (Hyndford Close or Fountain Close) to the **Museum of Childhood**, full of dolls and other toys, which possibly has more appeal for adults than for children.

The next junction marks the start of **Canongate** ❺. Two interesting museums are located in this section of the Royal Mile: first, the **People's Story Museum** in the picturesque building that was once the court prison, Canongate Tollbooth. Here the social history of Edinburgh is reconstructed from the standpoint of the working population by means of authentically furnished rooms, photographs and everyday objects. Huntly House on the other side of the road provides an insight into the history of the city with prehistoric, Roman and Celtic finds, craft objects and portraits. A passage next to Huntly House leads into one of the best-preserved courtyards in the city, Bakehouse Close. Some of the closes leading off Canongate are well worth investigating: tucked away in Lochend Close, for example, is Panmure House, where the economist Adam Smith lived until his death in 1790.

★★ **Holyroodhouse** ❻, at the bottom end of Canongate, is the official Scottish residence of the Queen. The palace was originally the Abbey guesthouse and the present building was completed around 1671. The areas open to the public are the State Apartments, the Picture Gallery and the Historic Apartments of Mary Stuart.

Holyroodhouse

A magnificent view of the New Town can be obtained from ★ **Calton Hill** ❼. On top of this hill is a collection of unusual buildings: the Nelson Monument, which can be climbed for yet another panoramic view (there is a small admission charge), the buildings of the City Observatory, only accessible by appointment, and the National Monument, which was never completed. Its proud creators, who built it as a memorial to fallen soldiers, intended it to become even more famous than the Parthenon of Athens on which it was modelled. The original, they declared in 1825, would be destroyed all too soon by the ravages of time and barbarianism, while their creation would survive. But unfortunately, in 1829 they ran out of money.

Piper in Princes Street

Walk down from Calton Hill along Waterloo Place and past the main station into ★ **Princes Street** ❽. On the right-hand side the shop fronts may spoil the effect of the Georgian architecture but this is more than compensated for by the park on the left-hand side with the Scott Monument and the precipitous Castle Rock as a back drop. When James Craig designed the New Town, he created

Calton Hill Observatory

three long axes (with George Street in the middle) and deliberately left the outer sides open (the north side of Queen Street and the south side of Princes Street).

Strolling in Charlotte Square

Where Princes Street is joined by The Mound there is a spacious square, the location of the **Royal Scottish Academy** of art, sculpture and architecture and the ★★ **National Gallery of Scotland** ❾. The National Gallery dates from the mid-19th century, and has been extended considerably. The collection of paintings is one of the most important in Europe – in addition to pictures by world-famous artists from Raphael to Rembrandt it includes major works by Scottish artists (*see page 79*).

Parallel to Princes Street is George Street, at the eastern end of which is ★★ **Charlotte Square** ❿. Designed in 1791 by Robert Adam, this is a masterpiece of Scottish neoclassical architecture. The Georgian House, has been furnished in period style and is open to the public.

The National Portrait Gallery

To the north of Charlotte Square is Queen Street, with the ★ **Royal Museum of Scotland** ⓫ containing archaeological and art collections and the ★ **National Portrait Gallery** at the far end. Beyond lies the 19th century extension of the New Town with its elegant squares and residences. Moray Place and the Royal Circus are especially worth a visit; the design and individual architecture of these two circles of houses reflect the status of their original middle-class owners.

The Royal Botanic Gardens

After crossing the **Water of Leith**, the city's main river (with an attractive riverside path) there is no better place to end an exploration of Edinburgh than the ★ **Royal Botanic Gardens** ⓬. They not only contain one of the major botanical collections in the world (including magnificent rhododendrons) but they are also a place where people go to relax – the lawns are there to be walked on. In addition to the famous Victorian Palm House, another building in the park which is worth a look is Inverleith House, a Georgian country mansion dating from 1774, which is now used for exhibitions. The Botanic Gardens Cafeteria near the house has good food and a wonderful view from the tables outside.

Excursion

Leith, Edinburgh's harbour to the northeast of the city, has a picturesque atmosphere which is all its own. Following the decline of merchant shipping the village, in particular the harbour quarter, went through a long period of unemployment and neglect, but has now re-emerged as a fashionable area. The street known as Shore on the banks of the Water of Leith where it flows into the harbour, has a number of inviting restaurants and pubs, while on the other side of the river is the Customs House, an interesting building dating from the early 19th century.

Glasgow Italian Centre

Route 2

★★ Glasgow

'Edinburgh is Scottish, Glasgow is cosmopolitan', wrote author H.V. Morton in the 1920s, and the distinction is still valid today. Until well after the beginning of the 20th century Glasgow was not only the harbour from which Scots set sail to make new lives in other lands. It was also the entry point for numerous immigrants from Ireland, Italy, India, Pakistan and other countries. Unlike Edinburgh, Glasgow was never able to pride itself on a glorious past, and the vitality for which it is famed was often paid for with social revolution and economic crises. Even today many visitors are initially surprised to find it is not a huge slum full of drunken rowdies.

In the last few years Glasgow has made a big effort to improve its image, and its new outlook was given a massive boost when the city was chosen European Cultural Capital in 1990. But nothing can change the fact that it is an industrial port with a high rate of unemployment. While there are no overall architectural characteristics, the city does have some of the most important art nouveau buildings in Europe (Glasgow style), magnificent architecture from the Victorian economic boom years, several museums of international repute – and charming people. In the words of the journalist Ian Nairn in 1960, 'Glasgow is without a doubt the friendliest city in Britain...' a fact which continues to delight its visitors.

Making music in Sauchiehall Street

Some cosmopolitan flair

History

The first church in Glasgow was built in the 6th century on the site of the present cathedral. It formed part of a monastery founded by St Mungo (also called Kentigern), the patron saint of the city, which became the centre of a steadily growing settlement. In 1175 *Glas cau* (the green place) was granted market rights by William the Lion and developed into an important trading centre. In 1451 it acquired a university (the second oldest in Scotland), but Glasgow was still a small place, and its religious and academic institutions were much more important than the town itself. For this reason it features scarcely at all in the history of Scotland's rulers, except as the place where Mary Stuart lost her last battle (in Langside) in 1568. Medieval castles or aristocratic palaces are conspicuous by their absence.

The Clyde today

From 1700 onwards, through the combination of a natural harbour and the requirements of the new heavy industries, Glasgow's economy began to grow. Maritime trade with America (in particular tobacco and cotton) created a need for shipbuilding, which was revolutionised by iron, steel and coal-fuelled steam engines. By 1913 the shipyards on the Clyde were making almost a third of

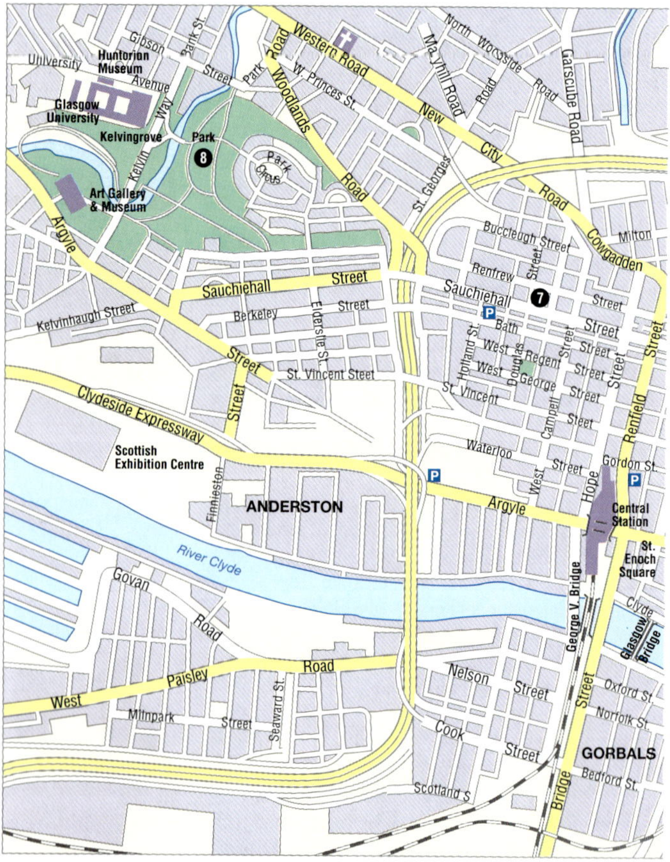

the world's steamships. The necessary labour came from the Highlands and Ireland: in 1780 Glasgow was a city with a population of 43,000; by 1861 it was almost ten times this size (396,000), and in 1901 it had 762,000 inhabitants – approximately the same number as it has today. Every economic crisis during the 19th century brought an increase in the number of people living in the notorious slums: one of the richest cities in the British Empire, it was also the one with the most acute social problems. The pompous Victorian architecture and the cramped estates of terraced houses, built at the same time, reflect this dichotomy.

The decline of heavy industry in Britain since the end of the 1960s hit Glasgow particularly hard, and it is only more recently that the negative image of drunkenness and unemployment has begun to fade as a result of the wide range of regenerative measures and cultural activities introduced by the city council.

Princes Square shopping mall

In Reuken Glen park

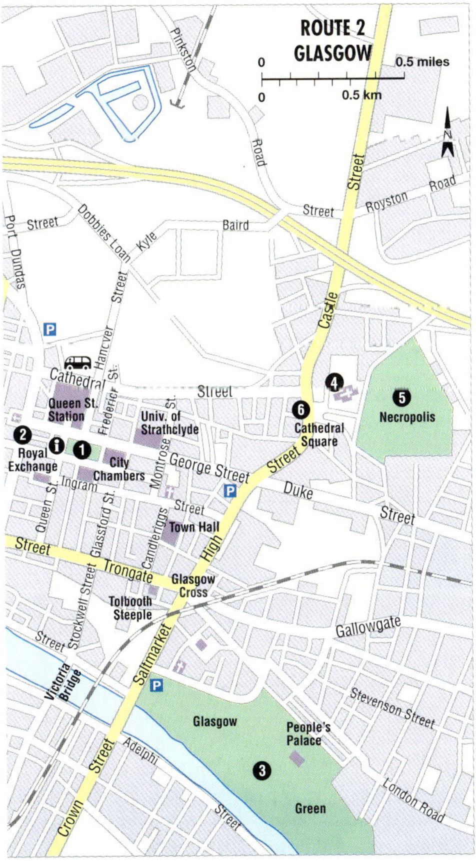

Buchanan Street is famous for shopping

The City Chambers

Sights

To understand what Glasgow was like in its Victorian heyday, begin your tour on ★ **George Square ❶**. The layout of this spacious square is typically Victorian, with an interesting selection of statues and monuments: in addition to the dominant figure of Sir Walter Scott on his 79-ft (24-metre) column there are (among others) statues of chemist Thomas Graham, publisher Thomas Campbell, politicians Robert Peel, William Gladstone and James Oswald, Lord Clyde, a general, and engineer James Watt (all erected in the 19th century). And, of course, there is Queen Victoria and Prince Albert. The east side of the square is taken up by the monumental town hall, the City Chambers, designed by the architect William Young in 1883–8 to the plan of a Roman Renaissance church, with facades modelled variously on Venetian and Roman styles. If you are impressed by the outside, take a look in the entrance hall, which Young called the Loggia, and which demonstrates that he did not believe in half measures.

★ **Buchanan Street ❷**, some of it a pedestrian precinct, is Glasgow's finest shopping street. In addition to Frasers department store and the Highland House of Lawrie, the famous supplier of traditional Scottish dress, the Princes Square shopping centre has the most elegant and fashionable shops in the city. At the southern end of this road is Argyll Arcade with its numerous jewellers, and on the other side of Argyle Street is the new shopping centre on St Enoch Square, not far from Glasgow's largest bookshop John Smith's (in St Vincent Street).

Footbridge over the Clyde

Walk down from St Enoch Square towards the Clyde and take the footbridge on the left to cross over to the riverside path, which leads past the former fish market, an imposing building dating from 1873, with colonnaded doorways, which is now full of shops and stalls.

This route leads to **Glasgow Green** ❸. In the 18th century this park was used for grazing and was also the place where the cotton dyers habitually spread their material out to dry; the present park was laid out in 1815. At its centre is the delightful museum known as the **People's Palace.** Built in 1893–8 'for the recreation and education of the population of Glasgow's East End', it now houses collections and exhibitions documenting the social history of the city, which is also the theme of the large mural painted by Ken Currie. Here the spirit of Glasgow comes alive: exhibits covering the battle for female suffrage and equality, the workers' movement, daily life during the two world wars, the Glasgow Style, Victoriana, the punk movement and much more besides show how the city became what it is today. The huge conservatory made of cast iron and glass adjoining the back of the People's Palace contains not only tropical plants but also a tea room and a stage.

The People's Palace

North of the park, the area between London Road and Gallowgate is transformed every weekend indoors and out by the largest ★ **fleamarket** in Scotland, a Glasgow institution and a great experience. On Saturday and Sunday the barrows spread out over the whole district, which swarms with tourists, local bargain-hunters and characters who may or may not be as genuine as they look. In the same area (mainly in the streets behind Bridgegate) is Paddy's Market, held from Monday to Saturday, and primarily used by the poorer sections of the population as a way of making a bit of cash.

The Barras fleamarket

The ★★ **Cathedral Church of St Mungo** ❹ is the official name of Glasgow Cathedral, uphill from the northern end of High Street. With its impressive exterior this 13th-century Gothic building is the most important Scottish church from this period. In the crypt are fragments of even older churches. From the outside the **Necropolis** ❺, on the hill behind the cathedral (modelled on the Paris cemetery Père Lachaise) is an untidy jumble of Victorian monuments. Until recently it was still possible to come here for a romantic view of the city framed by obelisks and angels of death, but the authorities have now declared it unsafe and closed it indefinitely. **Provand's Lordship** ❻ opposite the church, built for a priest in 1471, is today a museum documenting the history of Glasgow.

St Mungo's

The first stretch of Sauchiehall Street would be a perfectly ordinary pedestrian precinct with department stores if it were not for the 'Room de Luxe', the Willow Tea Rooms, which have been recreated on the first floor of Henderson's Gift Shop. Decorated throughout in lilac and silver, the interior has affinities with the 'Glasgow Style' founded by Charles Rennie Mackintosh. Mackintosh, who was born in 1868, was one of the foremost art nouveau architects and designers in Europe. On the left-hand side

Glasgow School of Art

Glasgow Art Gallery and Museum, inside and out

University of Glasgow

of Dalhousie Street, downhill from Sauchiehall Street, is the ★★ **Glasgow School of Art** ❼, his greatest achievement. The older side of the building, the east side, is reminiscent of the massive architecture of Scottish castles, while the long facade with its main entrance in Renfrew Street is less severe, and the west wing with its vertical window niches, designed in 1907 (ten years after the east side), looks positively modern. Mackintosh acknowledged that he enjoyed designing the interiors of buildings more than the exteriors, and the superb library is evidence of his genius. The building is still being used as it was intended, as an art academy, and it is not always possible to visit the rooms and the collection of sketches and watercolours without an appointment. The times of guided tours can be obtained from the Tourist Information Centre (*see page 96*). Information on the Glasgow Style of Mackintosh can also be obtained from the Charles Rennie Mackintosh Society in Queen's Cross Church (Garscube Rd), which Mackintosh also designed.

Sauchiehall Street runs right through the inner city. To the north on the other side of the urban motorway is Kelvingrove Park ❽ and the impressive 19th-century residential complex consisting of Park Gate, Park Circus, Park Terrace and Park Quadrant. It is primarily the work of Charles Wilson (1854), with individual buildings designed by other famous architects of the time. This was where the most influential families of Glasgow lived and on the southern edge of the park they built their temple to the arts, the ★★ **Glasgow Art Gallery and Museum**. Its collections are as fine as any in the national museums of Edinburgh: in addition to world-famous works by artists from Botticelli to Dali there is an excellent selection of works by 19th-century Scottish artists – most of the avant-gardists amongst them lived and worked in Glasgow. The museum would not of course be complete without a room devoted to the work of Charles Rennie Mackintosh.

But this is by no means the final example of the Glasgow Style: north of the museum, to the left of Kelvin Way, the broad footpath through the park, is the Victorian campus of the **University of Glasgow**. The modern visitor may detect no major difference between the style of the main building and the grand buildings of the period elsewhere in the city, but in 1863–4 there was a fierce dispute when the commission to design it went to the English architect George Gilbert Scott, who, adding insult to injury, also gave the building contract to an English firm.

Also part of the university is the **Hunterian Museum**, based on the collections of curiosities, fossils and coins of a professor of medicine called William Hunter. This museum with its famous coin collection has won several prizes: check whether there are any special exhibitions

here while you are in Glasgow. The ★ **Hunterian Art Gallery** consists of a collection of paintings and prints which was also started by Hunter but was continued after his death (and includes numerous works by Whistler and prints by Gauguin, Cezanne, Picasso, Kandinsky and Warhol). Mackintosh House is part of the complex and has reconstructed rooms from Mackintosh's own home.

Pollok House and gardens

Excursion

For an old industrial city Glasgow has a surprising number of open spaces, competing with London for the distinction of being the city with the largest park area relative to its size. On the far side of the once notorious areas, the Gorbals and Govan (with the Glasgow Rangers football stadium, Ibrox Park), south of the river, is the largest of the parks, the 363-acre (147-hectare) **Pollok Park**. The site of two important buildings with equally important art collections, Pollok Park is also very popular on fine days when Glaswegians picnic and enjoy the sun.

The two museums could not be more different from each other. The ★★ **Burrell Collection** in its prize-winning modern building is a conglomeration of precious objects from the collection of the magnate Charles Burrell. He invested his fortune in Chinese porcelain, antiques from the Mediterranean, Persian carpets and craftwork from medieval Europe. When he left it all to the city in 1944 he was concerned about the effects of industrial pollution on his treasures and stipulated that they be accommodated at least 15 miles (25km) outside the city. It was only in 1967 that his heirs agreed to have the collection housed in Pollok Park. This had just been made over to the city by Mrs Anne Maxwell Macdonald, together with ★★ **Pollok House**, the neoclassical mansion belonging to her family, complete with its collection of Spanish paintings, including works by El Greco, Murillo and Goya).

The Burrell

Route 3

Aberdeen

For centuries Aberdeen was a centre of world trade, but today it is rather off the beaten track. Travellers must make a deliberate decision to visit it: it is nowhere near the main routes through the Highlands, and there are miles of open countryside to be driven through before reaching the unprepossessing outlying districts of the city with its minor industries and suburban estates. And when looking for accommodation visitors soon discover that the city is more interested in North Sea oil than in tourists. While Edinburgh is besieged by weekend visitors, the hotels of Aberdeen are full during the week and advertise special offers at weekends.

However, the city is now promoting itself as a family holiday resort, and has plenty to offer the visitor: a distinctive appearance compounded of granite buildings and flower beds; a long and varied history; several excellent museums and a glimpse of the branch of Scottish industry which since 1975 has been keeping the whole British economy going.

A city of granite

History

Aberdeen's ideal location at the mouth of the River Dee, with its natural harbour, made it an obvious place for settlement, and prehistoric settlers. Romans and Picts are known to have established themselves on this site. In the year 1136, because of its significance as a port, Aberdeen was granted the right to collect shipping duties, and in 1179 it became a Royal Burgh. In 1336–37 Edward III of England burned it to the ground and it was subsequently rebuilt on a much larger scale.

Formal attire at Marischal College

The importance of Aberdeen can be measured by the fact that in 1495 it already had a university, the third oldest in Scotland. In subsequent centuries the city flourished as a major fishing and trading port, and was also the largest cattle market north of the Firth of Forth – the farmers drove their animals here from as far away as the remote Highlands of Wester Ross. During the Jacobite Risings of 1715 and 1745 the city officially supported the rebels, but kept its options open for the sake of peace and trade.

In the 18th and 19th centuries colonial trade and the textile industry made Aberdeen prosperous. The harbour had to be enlarged and in 1869, as a consequence, the Dee was diverted – in those days an unprecedented undertaking. Exactly a hundred years later the next major restructuring of the harbour took place in order to provide berths for modern ferries and the ships supplying the North Sea oil rigs. With the oil boom the city regained its key position in the economic life of Scotland.

Attracting shoppers

Harbour facilities

Sights

The **harbour** ❶ is the city's focal point and its main source of income. It is accessible to visitors although some caution is advised. Early risers can experience the hustle and bustle as the night's catch is auctioned (before 7.30am) in the modern fish market on Albert Basin (Market Street). The history of the harbour is clearly documented in the ★ **Maritime Museum** ❷ in Provost Ross's house on Shiprow north of the Upper Dock. The house is interesting in itself – it was built in 1593 as the home of a wealthy merchant.

The inner city north of the harbour is dominated by two gigantic shopping centres, the Bon Accord Centre and the St Nicholas Centre. The **Kirk of St Nicholas** ❸ dates in part from the 12th century. During the Reformation the church was divided and used by both Catholics and Protestants. In the 17th century the crypt of the eastern part was used for the imprisonment of women accused of witchcraft, who were attached by chains to the iron rings that can still be seen in the wall.

The ★**Aberdeen Art Gallery and Museum** ❹ on the corner of Blackfriars Street and Schoolhill has an impressive collection of European paintings mainly from the 18th to the 20th centuries as well as works by a number of contemporary Scottish artists; the collection of Scottish silver and glass is also well worth seeing. ★ **Provost Skene's House** ❺ in Flourmill Lane, built in 1545 and the oldest house in the city, seems something of an anachronism crowded out by the shopping centres and office blocks. It has been carefully restored and is now a museum with rooms decorated in the style of its various occupants down the centuries.

ROUTE 3
ABERDEEN
0 0.25 miles
0 0.3 km
River Don
Fraserburgh
Bridge o'Don
Don Street
Kettocks Mill Road
Kettocks Mill
Seaton Park
Wallace Tower
Tillydrone Road
Harris Drive
Tillydrone Av.
Botanical Gardens
Chanonry
Wingate Road
King Street
SEATON
Seaton Dr.
King's Links
Beach Esplanade
St. Machar Drive
School Road
Golf Course
University
High Street
Meston Walk
King's College
Regent Walk
Bedford Road
Bedford Av.
University Rd
OLD ABERDEEN
Golf Road
Linksfield Road
Sunnyside Road
Orchard St.
Inverness
Elmfield Av.
Spital
Merkland Street
Pittodrie Park
Elmbank Terr.
Froghall Terr.
Powis Place
Kings Cr.
Seaforth Road
Holland Street
George Street
Nelson Street
Urquhart Road
Hutcheon Street
West North Street
Jasmine T.
Codona's Amusement Park
Skene Square
Maberley St.
Rosemount Place
Park Street
Constitution Street
Beach Boulevard
Gallowgate
John St.
Baker St.
S. Mount St.
Bon Accord Centre
Kirkgate
Upper Broad St.
St. Andrews Cath.
Links Road
Rosemount Viaduct
School Hill
Justice St.
Commerce St.
Miller St.
Town House
Virginia St.
Skene St.
Union Terr.
St. Clement St.
Huntly Street
Regent Quay
Waterloo Quay
Wellington Street
York St.
Union Street
Trinity Quay
Market Street
Upper Dock
Victoria Dock
Guild Street
Bridge St.
Blaikies Quay
Crown Street
Guild Street Station
Fish Market
Commercial Quay
Stonehaven
Albert Basin
1
2
3
4
5
6
7
8
P

30

★★ **Marischal College** on Broad Street was founded in 1593 in competition with the Catholic King's College. Rebuilt at the end of the 19th century, it has the distinction of being the second largest granite building in the world, after the Escorial Palace in Madrid. The extraordinary fretwork of pinnacles and gilt flags on the neo-Gothic facade make the unyielding substance of white granite seem almost delicate. One of the sections of the **University of Aberdeen Anthropological Museum** ❻ that is accommodated inside has exhibits relating to the prehistoric inhabitants of Scotland, in particular from the area around Aberdeen.

George Street or King Street, the main road which runs north behind Marischal College, will bring you to Old Aberdeen. On the parallel road, High Street, is **King's College**, the older of the two university colleges. The chapel dates from 1500 and contains the tomb of the university's founder, Bishop Elphinstone, to whom there is also a memorial in front of the building.

★ **St Machar's Cathedral** ❼ is the oldest granite building in Aberdeen, which is often called 'Granite City'. It is worth taking a leisurely stroll though the area around the church with its old town houses, cobbled streets and air of unruffled solidity. The area extends to the ★ **Brig o' Balgownie** ❽ over the River Don, the oldest Gothic bridge in Scotland, which is inevitably associated with a variety of legends. The popular hero Robert Bruce is said to have ordered its construction personally, and the mystic seer Thomas the Rhymer to have prophesied that it would collapse if a father with an only son ever rode across it on the only foal of a mare. Lord Byron, who went to school in Aberdeen, owned that as an only child he was afraid to cross the bridge.

King's College

Brig o' Balgownie

Excursion

Of the many aristocratic houses in the Aberdeen area **Crathes Castle** is probably the most popular (house, Easter to October, daily from 11am; garden, all year from 9.30am). It is easily accessible on the A93 and it has all the necessary attributes of a 'typical Scottish castle': built in 1553–94 with picturesque battlements it not only has three rooms with impressive ceiling paintings in the typical Scottish style but also a collection of ghosts, including the Green Lady. She is said to appear with her child – an infant skeleton was found underneath the fireplace in one of the rooms she occupied.

The delightful gardens cover an area of 593 acres (240 hectares) and are divided up into separate sections. They are as popular with Aberdonians as with tourists, and visitors are well catered for with a café, information centre and souvenir shop.

Crathes Castle

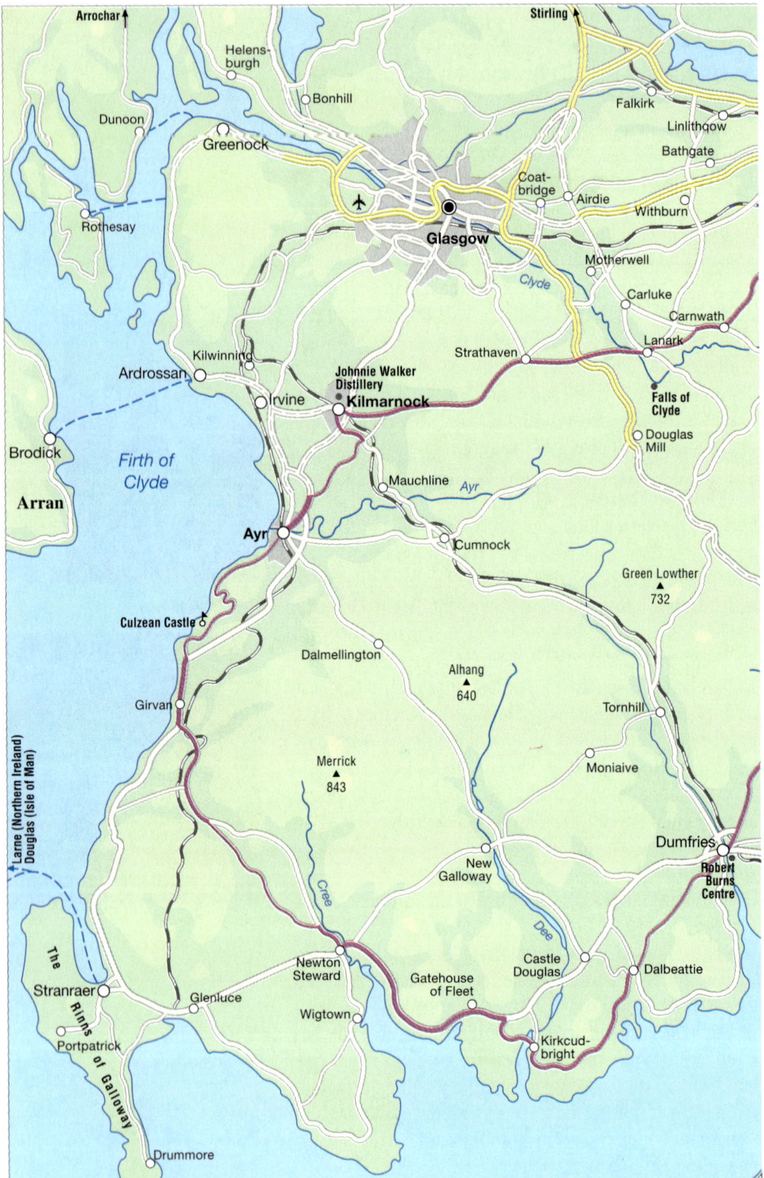
Arrochar
Stirling
Helensburgh
Bonhill
Falkirk
Linlithgow
Dunoon
Greenock
Bathgate
Coatbridge
Airdie
Withburn
Rothesay
Glasgow
Motherwell
Clyde
Carluke
Carnwath
Lanark
Strathaven
Kilwinning
Ardrossan
Johnnie Walker Distillery
Kilmarnock
Irvine
Falls of Clyde
Brodick
Douglas Mill
Firth of Clyde
Mauchline
Ayr
Arran
Ayr
Cumnock
Green Lowther
732
Culzean Castle
Dalmellington
Alhang
640
Girvan
Tornhill
Merrick
843
Moniaive
Larne (Northern Ireland)
Douglas (Isle of Man)
Dumfries
New Galloway
Robert Burns Centre
Cree
Dee
The Rinns of Galloway
Newton Steward
Castle Douglas
Dalbeattie
Stranraer
Gatehouse of Fleet
Glenluce
Wigtown
Portpatrick
Kirkcudbright
Drummore
Workington

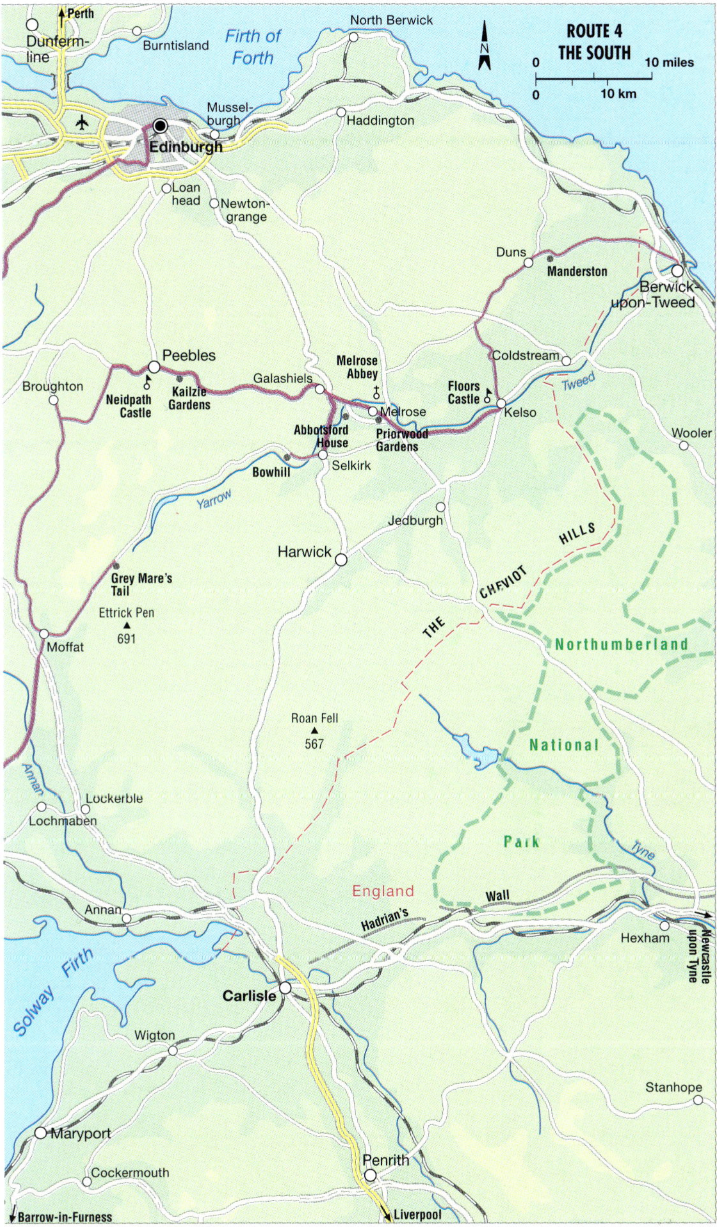
ROUTE 4
THE SOUTH
0 10 miles
0 10 km
N
Perth
Dunferm-line
Burntisland
Firth of Forth
North Berwick
Mussel-burgh
Haddington
Edinburgh
Loan head
Newton-grange
Duns
Manderston
Berwick-upon-Tweed
Coldstream
Tweed
Peebles
Broughton
Neidpath Castle
Kailzie Gardens
Galashiels
Melrose Abbey
Floors Castle
Kelso
Melrose
Abbotsford House
Priorwood Gardens
Wooler
Selkirk
Bowhill
Yarrow
Jedburgh
Harwick
Grey Mare's Tail
Ettrick Pen
691
THE CHEVIOT HILLS
Moffat
Northumberland
National
Park
Roan Fell
567
Annan
Lockerbie
Lochmaben
Tyne
England
Wall
Hadrian's
Annan
Hexham
Newcastle upon Tyne
Solway Firth
Carlisle
Wigton
Stanhope
Maryport
Penrith
Cockermouth
Barrow-in-Furness
Liverpool

St Mary's Loch near Moffat

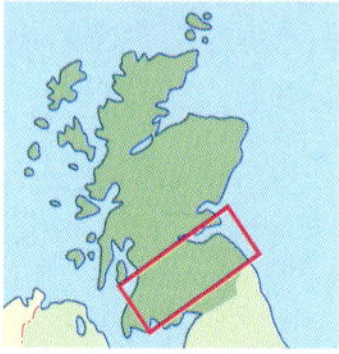

Route 4

The South *See map on pages 32–3*

The Borders – Dumfries and Galloway – Ayrshire

In past centuries the Scottish border sometimes ran well south of the little town of Berwick-upon-Tweed on the North Sea coast, over which many battles were fought and which is now part of England. The traveller will certainly notice no radical changes in the landscape when crossing the border on the North Sea coast. The gently rolling hills only give way to more dramatic landscape further to the west. The ruins of numerous castles and abbeys are a reminder of the constant disputes between the English and the Scots, but in around 1800 they had a romantic attraction for two of Scotland's most famous poets, both of whom settled in this area. Robert Burns spent the first years of his life in and around Ayr and his last years in Dumfries, while Walter Scott settled in Abbotsford House near Melrose.

The following route describes an arc from the east coast through the Southern Uplands to the Irish Sea in the west and returns in a northeasterly direction to Edinburgh. It is best followed by car or by bicycle: there were once good bus services in the area but they have been cut back considerably in recent years. The route description includes a few pleasant detours on foot and indicates where there are footpaths.

Many visitors to Scotland are in such a hurry to get to the spectacular scenery of the famous Highlands that they simply pass this region by. But the south has a great deal to offer, and we can only discourage you from following their example.

Maintaining the memory of Burns

Sir Walter Scott in Selkirk

The Great North Road from London to Edinburgh, otherwise known as the A1, crosses the Scottish border north of Berwick-upon-Tweed. This is the moment to leave the main road – to the west are the **Lammermuir Hills** with quiet minor roads through narrow valleys between high moorland hills.

One of the attractions on the southern edge of the Lammermuir Hills is **Manderston House** near Duns (May to September, Thursday and Sunday 2–5.30pm). It is a very fine example of an Edwardian country house dating from the early 20th century, although its severe neoclassical proportions actually go back to the end of the 18th century. The hemp and herring millionaire Sir James Miller who acquired it in 1900 only made a few alterations and extensions – the opulent marble cladding (even in the stables), silver bannisters and spacious servants' quarters are all evidence of a degree of luxury that must have seemed completely anachronistic only a few years later. The extensive gardens contribute to the overall, lavish impression – as so often in Scottish gardens, rhododendrons are the speciality.

Kelso is a typical small border town with a large market square at its centre. It is famous for its ruined **abbey**, located next to the parish church. This was once the largest and richest of the medieval abbeys in the southeast (the others being Dryburgh, Jedburgh and Melrose), of which only ruins remain. They were all destroyed in the 16th century either during the dissolution of the monasteries ordered by Henry VIII or the subsequent religious wars and wars of succession. Today, Kelso abbey is the least complete of all of them.

Floors Castle, almost 2 miles (3km) northwest of Kelso (April to June and September, Sunday to Thursday from 10.30am, July and August, daily from 10.30am, October, Sunday and Wednesday from 10.30am) is the magnificent country seat of the Dukes of Roxburghe. The house, begun in 1721 by William Adam and considerably enlarged in the 19th century, is the largest inhabited castle in Scotland and became well-known all over the world when it featured as Tarzan's ancestral home in the Hollywood film *Greystoke*. There is a splendid view over the Tweed; the hill on the far side of the river was the site of one of the largest medieval fortresses in Scotland – although the little that remains of Roxburgh Castle is now barely visible from this distance.

To escape the crowds at Floors Castle, turn left off the road to the castle and head for the river. The grass-covered banks where the local people traditionally go to picnic and swim in the Tweed are known as The Cobby. Visitors should only venture into the river for a refreshing dip if they are strong swimmers.

Features of Floors Castle

By the banks of the Tweed

Melrose Abbey

Abbotsford House – Scott's dream

In this area it is impossible not to come into contact with the Roxburghe family: they own the best hotel for miles around, Sunlaws House, on the A698 at Heiton, 3 miles (5km) south of Kelso. The Victorian country house looks so imposing that most people assume it will be out of their price range – but anyone who is not on a very restricted budget should make inquiries and might be pleasantly surprised. The food here is first class and there are reasonably priced bar lunches.

★★ **Melrose** is famous mainly for its ruined **abbey** (Monday to Saturday from 9.30am, Sunday from 2pm). The Cistercian monastery, founded in 1136, is in a more romantic setting than Kelso Abbey and has the added attraction of the adjoining **Priorwood Gardens** (April to December, Monday to Saturday from 10am, Sunday from 1.30pm). On the other side of its high walls is a garden where flowers and plants are grown for drying and pressing; the shop also sells homemade jelly produced from the traditional varieties of apple grown in the adjacent orchard.

Abbotsford House, 2 miles (3km) west of Melrose (March to October, Monday to Saturday from 10am, Sunday from 2pm) is the country seat that Sir Walter Scott had always wanted; he designed it himself and spent the last 20 years of his life here. The house makes a romantic impression, from the pseudo-medieval magnificence of the entrance hall to the inviting library with its many valuable tomes from Scott's own collection. It is easy to imagine him writing *Waverley, Ivanhoe* and *Kenilworth* here and in the neighbouring study. Some of these works were produced in a great hurry – his generosity as a host and his attempts to establish himself as a member of the landed gentry meant that he was constantly short of money and needed to keep producing books.

For an overnight stop it is worth making a detour to **Selkirk**. The place itself is typical of the Borders, and unremarkable save for the fact that Sir Walter Scott was sheriff (judge) here for more than 30 years. The court (today the Town Hall) dominates the market square and naturally has a collection of Scott memorabilia.

An alternative overnight stop is the **Philipburn House Hotel**, at the junction of the A707 and A798. It is not cheap, but a delight for two categories of people who are often rather neglected – children and vegetarians. Philipburn House has family suites, an extensive garden with playgrounds and swimming pool, a children's menu, and friendly, helpful staff. Vegetarians need only glance at the menu (which has plenty of meat dishes as well), and wine connoisseurs at the wine menu to known that they have come to the right place.

Bowhill (3 miles/5km west of Selkirk on the A708) is also a delight for children and young people, and for art lovers of any age (house, July only, Monday to Saturday from noon, Sunday from 1pm; garden, April to August at the same times). The 18th-century estate is one of the many properties of the Dukes of Buccleuch, who are the richest landowners in Scotland, and like all the family's houses it is overflowing with treasures. In addition to the famous collection of portrait miniatures there are important paintings by Raeburn, Gainsborough, Reynolds, Canaletto, Guardi, Claude Lorrain, Leonardo da Vinci and Ruysdael. There are also Louis-Quinze chairs with Aubusson covers, Meissen porcelain, hand-painted 18th-century Chinese wallpaper and much more besides. Younger members of the family, who are soon bored by all this splendour, are catered for with an adventure playground containing wonderful tree houses, a riding stable, bicycles for hire and special paths for their use, footpaths to the nearby loch and the romantic ruin of Newark Castle, and the Bowhill Little Theatre next to the house, with a tiny stage and a varied programme. And if this is not sufficient, there is also a souvenir shop and a tearoom.

★ **Peebles on the Tweed** is a tourist centre, but this by no means diminishes its attractions. Whether you pause en route to shop or visit a café (The Sunflower or Gino's Café de Luxe near the bridge), stay overnight in the vast Peebles Hydro hotel, or go for a walk in the Kailzie Garden or the Dawyck Botanic Garden, along the Tweed by the magnificently sited Neidpath Castle, or wander into Cardrona Forest, you will not regret the time spent here.

Popular Peebles

Peebles Hydro and similar establishments are reminders that until well into the 19th century there were many spa towns in this area. In **Moffat**, for example, there is a well preserved bathhouse. But this friendly place on the road south to the Dumfries coast is best known for the Toffee Shop on its spacious market square, where the world-famous Moffat Toffee is made and sold. This creamy confectionery is sold as sweets, but the real addicts buy it in bars. From Moffat it is worth making a detour to the ★ **Grey Mare's Tail**, a spectacular waterfall 10 miles (16km) to the northeast with a fine walk around it. The A708 from Selkirk to Moffat, past the waterfall and St Mary's Loch (where a stop at Tibbie Shiels Inn is a must), is one of the most beautiful roads in the area.

The Grey Mare's Tail

Dumfries is the largest town in the Scottish southwest, with a population of 32,000, and is also the administrative centre of the Dumfries and Galloway region. Due to its location it was formerly a place of strategic importance: several times in its history it was invaded and destroyed. Today it is a major junction, a shopping centre and one

A Dumfries institution

Burns's bed

of the focal points of the tourist industry that has been generated around the Scottish national poet, Robert Burns. Burns spent the last six years of his life in Dumfries, and his memory is kept alive by ★ **Burns House**, where he died in 1796, by the mausoleum over his grave in the cemetery of St Michael, the statue in the High Street, the memorabilia in his favourite pubs, the Globe Tavern and the Hole in the Wall, and in particular by the **Robert Burns Centre** in Mill Road (April to September, Monday to Saturday from 10am, Sunday from 2pm; October to March, Tuesday to Saturday from 10am). In the former mill there are audio-visual displays, models and other exhibits illustrating the life and work of the poet, as well as information about the other stations on the 'Burns Trail'.

For an overnight stay and a decent meal, the Station Hotel is a good, plain, reasonably priced establishment.

South of Dumfries is the beautiful coast on the **Solway Firth**, which is reasonably quiet, though swimming might not be advisable owing to the high levels of radiation in the sea emanating from the Sellafield reprocessing plant 31 miles (50 km) to the south, on the Cumbrian coast.

A good road (A701/A711) takes you along the coast to Kirkcudbright, with some interesting features en route. While the ruins of **Sweetheart Abbey** in the village of New Abbey are not as monumental as those of Melrose in the Borders, they are well preserved, attractively sited and not quite as crowded as the more famous abbeys. The name goes back to the founder of the monastery, the pious (and rich) Devorguilla de Balliol, who was buried here in 1290 together with the embalmed heart of her beloved husband John. After his death at a young age she had carried his heart around with her in a silver box.

A little further off the main road is **Orchadton Tower** (signposted on the A711 south of Palnackie), the only round tower house in Scotland. It is thought to have been built in the 15th century by Irish builders, since Ireland has many such towers. The ruin is at first rather inconspicuous, as is its setting, but those who make the effort to climb the narrow winding staircase will not regret it.

In the village of Auchencairn turn down the single-track road to Balcary Bay Hotel. The whole coast was once a notorious smugglers' paradise, especially since the Isle of Man was outside the sphere of the British customs authorities until 1876. In the 18th century a commercial company established on the Isle of Man went so far as to build a supply cellar with a solid country house over it on this sheltered spot on the coast. Today this house is run as the Balcary Bay Hotel and at dusk, when staying in one of the fine rooms overlooking the bay, it is easy to imagine the smugglers' ships unloading their booty on the beach.

This route takes us finally to **Kirkcudbright**, pronounced 'Kirkubree', on the estuary of the River Dee. As you drive through the green park-like landscape into this spacious town on a sunny day, you may well wish that you could stay here for longer.

There are many prehistoric sites dotted along the Solway Coast, the most impressive of which is to be found west of Gatehouse of Fleet: follow the signs on the A75 and walk uphill through the woods to the graves of ★ **Cairnholy I and II**. Most people's first thought is that those who piled these stones one on top of the other 4,000 years ago must have been greatly in awe of death. A semicircle of upright stone slabs guards the narrow burial chamber of Cairnholy I, the entrance to which faces out over the open sea. During the excavations objects were found which must have been brought here from far away in Central and Southern Europe, including bell beakers and parts of an axe made of jadeite. The slab of rock on top of the burial chamber of Cairnholy II would have needed quite a number of men to carry it here.

Newton Stewart is a good centre for a holiday in this region with a good, quiet and reasonably priced hotel in the town itself (the Creebridge House Hotel). The peninsula to the south (The Machars) has two picturesque towns, **Wigtown** and **Whithorn**, beautiful beaches, peaceful countryside and numerous prehistoric and ancient sites. In addition to the Wren's Egg and Torhouse stone circles the excavations in Whithorn are particularly interesting. Whithorn Dig and Visitor Centre in George Street (Easter to October, Monday to Saturday from 10.30am) runs guided tours and an exhibition detailing the early Christian, Viking and medieval settlements.

North of Newton Stewart is the **Galloway Forest Park**, a nature reserve 249sq miles (645sq km) in area with good

Veteran of the times

Keeping Kirkcudbright clean

Canoeing on the Rhinns of Galloway…

…an area of great beauty

footpaths, a natural history information centre (Galloway Deer Museum at Clatteringshaws Loch), wild goat and deer enclosures and many other points of interest. There is even a special route for people who want to explore the forest without getting out of their car (Raiders Road, branching off the A712). West of Newton Stewart is ★ **The Rhinns of Galloway**. This peninsula, shaped like a hammerhead, is an area of great beauty with wide sandy beaches to the east and steep cliffs to the west, from which, on a clear day, it looks like Ireland is just a swim away.

From the coast road from Stranraer north towards Ayr (A77/A719) there are magnificent views of the sea and the 1,115-ft (340-m) granite cone of **Ailsa Craig Island**. Once the place to which insubordinate monks were sent, the island is now reserved for its rightful inhabitants, and has become a bird sanctuary (boat trips from Girvan).

The battlements of Culzean

In Scotland so many castles are a must on the tourist's list that it is difficult to find the right superlatives to do justice to ★★ **Culzean Castle** (April to October, daily from 10.30am). It is neither particularly large nor particularly old, particularly historic nor particularly spectacular. But to drive past it would be to miss something absolutely unique. At Culzean (pronounced 'Collane') between 1777 and 1792 Scotland's famous architect Robert Adam transformed a 16th-century tower house for the titled Kennedy family, producing an astonishing synthesis of neoclassical mansion and romantic castle. Although the exterior alone is well worth seeing, it is in the central staircase and the interior design of the rooms that Adam's genius is fully revealed. If all you ever see of Robert Adam's work is the wonderful circular drawing room with its ceiling in three pastel shades, you will nevertheless have a perfect idea of Scottish Enlightenment elegance. The 18th-century-style park is also worth a visit (all year from 9.30am).

The resorts on the coast between the Rhinns Peninsula and the Firth of Clyde, ranging from old-fashioned, rather conservative Troon with its famous golf courses to Saltcoats with its bingo halls, slot-machines and fairgrounds, become suburbs of Glasgow in the summer.

The largest of all these resorts is **Ayr**. The broad sandy beaches are well-kept and apparently accommodate with ease the thousands of tourists who come here in the main season. But this is not all there is to do here – golf is the second major attraction of the town, and there are three fine courses. Ayr also has the most famous racecourse in Scotland and is a focal point for Robert Burns' devotees: his birthplace, Alloway, is now a suburb in the southern part of the town. The well-marked **Burns Heritage Trail** leads to the house where he was born (now a museum) and other places associated with the poet's life. Maps and guides can be obtained from the Tourist Information Centre (*see page 97*).

The old bridge in Ayr

If sightseeing has made you hungry, Fouters Restaurant in Academy Street, opposite the information centre, is hard to beat. The restaurant itself is very sophisticated, but the adjoining bistro is less formal, with hardly any difference in the food. The Burns Monument Hotel in Alloway, close to the famous Burns House, is a pleasant place to stay, while for golfers Northpark House is ideal, located next to Belleisle, a frequently recommended course which is open to non-members.

Burns's birthplace

From Ayr almost all roads lead to Glasgow (A77) or Edinburgh (A71), but there is one more detour worth making: from the A72 turn off in the direction of Lanark to New Lanark and the **Falls of Clyde**. This is a popular destination for walkers. The scenery is straight out of a romantic painting, with the river tumbling over granite rocks and the oaks and birches leaning over it veiled in the spray from the falls.

★ **New Lanark** on the banks of the Clyde below the waterfall is an open-air museum (visitors' centre, all year from 11am). Here, in 1800, the industrialist David Dale and his son-in-law, reformer Robert Owen, embarked on what was then a revolutionary experiment: they set out to provide the workers in the cotton mills with proper housing, decent working conditions and educational facilities. 'When Robert Owen... went beyond theoretical support for a restriction of the working day to 10 hours and put it into practice in his factory in New Lanark, this was derided as communist utopian thinking, as was also the link he established between productive work and child education, and the workers' cooperative stores that he founded', Karl Marx later wrote. Today the settlement seems positively idyllic.

New Lanark

ROUTE 5
THE EAST
0
30 miles
0
30 km
N
NORTH SEA
Wick
Latheron
Branderburgh-
Lossiemouth
Cromarty
Elgin
Banff
Macduff
Fraserburgh
Nairn
Keith
Craigellachie
Spey
Findhorn
Culloden
Moor
Inverness
Loch Ness
Dufftown
Huntly
Peterhead
Speyside
Stone
Circle
Glenlivet
Inverurie
Orkney Islands
Tomintoul
Loch
Garten
Aviemore
Aberdeen
CAIRNGORMS
Ben Macdui
1309
Ben Avon
1171
Banchory
Dee
GRAMPIAN MOUNTAINS
Balmoral
Castle
Mt. Keen
938
Stonehaven
Dunnottar
Castle
Pass of
Drumochter
Fasque
Beinn-á Ghlo
1119
Angus
Pass of Killiecrankie
Pitlochry
House of
Dun
Montrose
Schiehallion
1081
Glamis
Castle
Forfar
Arbroath
Dundee
Perth
Firth of Tay
Crieff
R. Earn
St. Andrews
Falkland
Palace
Fife
Crail
Anstruther
Pittenweem
Stirling
Castle
Dollar
Kinross
Stirling
Dunfermline
Kirkcaldy
Firth of Forth
North Berwick
Burntisland
Falkirk
Linlithgow
Edinburgh
Haddington
Glasgow
Whitburn
Carlisle

Route 5

The East

Fife – Tayside – Grampian

There is no route through the eastern part of Scotland north of Edinburgh that does not reinforce the standard image of Scotland: golf, castles and whisky simply cannot be avoided. It is also in the east that the most famous names associated with each are to be found: the Old Course of St Andrews, Stirling Castle, Falkland Palace and the numerous distilleries of Speyside, the heartland of Scottish whisky production. With the idyllic stretches of coast and the grandiose mountain landscape of the Cairngorms also on offer, the area provides a selection of Scotland's best tourist attractions.

From Edinburgh, the route described below leads, with a detour to Stirling, along the coast of Fife with its picturesque fishing villages and then turns inland into the old county of Angus. South of Aberdeen it returns briefly to the North Sea, then bends round to the north, leading through the valleys of Speyside and finally up to Inverness. This is a classic holiday area (for the royal family as well as many of their subjects) and you are unlikely to find solitude. But the people who come here know what pleasures await them.

Defending Stirling Castle

It is hard to leave Edinburgh without getting caught up in the jumble of motorways, dormitory towns and industrial estates on the south bank of the Firth of Forth. But this uninviting-looking area is not without its attractions: the impressive ★★ **Forth Rail Bridge**, for example, built in 1883–90, is one of the greatest engineering achieve-

The Forth Rail Bridge

Inside Hopetoun House

Robert the Bruce at Bannockburn

A figure in Stirling's history

The castle walls

ments of its time and still a conspicuous monument to progressive Victorian thinking. It has also become the ultimate in never-ending tasks – when the painters with their red anti-rust paint reach the end of the bridge it is said that they have to start again immediately at the other end. A short distance to the west is ★★ **Hopetoun House** (Easter to September 10am–5pm) an interesting 18th-century manor house set in a large park on the banks of the Forth.

Proceed from here to the **Bannockburn Heritage Centre** in the suburbs of Stirling near the M9/M80 merging point. A rotunda with an equestrian statue next to it marks the spot where, in 1314, Robert Bruce marshalled the Scottish troops to lead them to their bloodiest victory over the English: 'two counts, more than 60 barons and standard bearers, 268 knights and no less than 10,000 foot soldiers' on the English side lost their lives and King Edward II was forced to flee. The Battle of Bannockburn is significant for nationally-minded Scots because it represented such a humiliating defeat for their arch enemy that it has become a symbol of Scottish independence.

North of the battlefield is the centre of **Stirling**. The town is dominated by ★ **Stirling Castle** (April to September, Monday to Saturday 9.30am–5.15pm, Sunday from 10.30am; October to March, Monday to Saturday 9.30am–4.30pm, Sunday from 12.30pm). Its impressive bulk immediately reminds one of Edinburgh, and it has an equally noble history: this royal residence saw the deaths of Alexander I (1124) and William the Lion (1214), the birth of James III in 1451 and the coronation of Mary Stuart as Queen of Scotland in 1543 at the age of nine months. Most of the present building dates from the 15th and 16th centuries – information about its history can be obtained in the Visitors' Centre on the Esplanade.

At the foot of the castle is the oldest and most attractive part of Stirling. In interesting buildings such as **Argyll's Lodging** and the Guildhall visitors are greeted during the main tourist season by people in historic costume who give 'first-hand' accounts of the building's past history and occupants. The street theatre performance called the Ghost Walk is even more interesting: every evening in the summer 'the world of restless spirits and lost souls' comes to life around the castle (family performance 7pm; a more bloodthirsty version at 9.30pm).

Argyll's Lodging

From Stirling, head east to the **Fife Peninsula**. On the southern side of the Ochil Hills is **Dollar**, with the romantic **Castle Campbell** (April to September, Monday to Saturday from 9.30am, Sunday from 2pm; October to March, closed Thursday afternoon and Friday) perched high above the woods of Dollar Glen. It is worth negotiating the steep climb up to the castle for the splendid view over the Forth Valley. The walks along the stream through the deciduous woods of the glen are particularly to be recommended in autumn, and for dedicated walkers there are longer trails through the Ochil Hills.

South of Auchtermuchty is Falkland with **Falkland Palace,** the hunting lodge of the Stuart dynasty (April to October, Monday to Saturday from 10am, Sunday from 2pm). The guided tour of the palace, which was built between 1501 and 1542, not only takes in the reception rooms and private apartments, but also includes an explanation of Royal Tennis which demonstrates that the complicated game of the kings has little more in common with modern tennis than the use of a strung racquet.

Falkland Palace

On the south coast of Fife is a string of attractive fishing villages, the largest of which is Anstruther, officially called the United Burgh of Kilrenny, Cellardyke, Anstruther Easter and Anstruther Wester, and referred to by the local people simply as Ainster. The **Scottish Fisheries Museum** on the harbour (April to October, Monday to Saturday from 10am, Sunday from 11am; November to March, Monday to Saturday from 10am, Sunday from 2pm) gives a good picture of the history and practice of fishing on this coast and also has two real fishing boats, which are moored next to the museum building. In summer there are boat trips from Anstruther to see the puffins on the **Isle of May**. The 3½-mile (6-km) coastal path from Anstruther to the picturesque harbour of Crail is also to be recommended (weary walkers can take the bus back).

Outside the Fisheries Museum

St Andrews is probably best known as the world-famous 'home of golf'. The Royal and Ancient Golf Club, founded in 1754, is the final authority on everything to do with

St Andrews, home of golf

the rules and history of the sport, and a visit to the **British Golf Museum** opposite the clubhouse (May to October, daily from 10am, November to April, closed Monday) is a must for golfing enthusiasts. Golf is naturally not all this attractive place has to offer: it has the oldest and most highly regarded university in Scotland, and students populate its streets. From the 10th century St Andrews was the seat of the most powerful bishop in Scotland, and had the largest cathedral in the country: the ruins of this building – ★★ **St Andrews Cathedral** at the end of South Street – still convey something of its former medieval splendour.

From St Andrews, head north, leaving the Peninsula of Fife via the Tay Bridge which which will take you to Dundee, the fourth largest city in Scotland. The two museum ships in the harbour are worth a visit: the *RRS Discovery* was the expedition ship of the South Pole explorer Robert Falcon Scott in 1901–04; the *HMS Unicorn* is a frigate with 46 cannons which was launched in 1824 – and illustrates only too well the appalling conditions that were endured by sailors of the time. Dundee could be described a little cynically as an endless suburb with a shopping centre in the middle – the architectural past has been obliterated more thoroughly here than elsewhere.

RSS Discovery

North of Dundee in the rolling hills of Angus (home of the famous breed of cattle) is **Glamis** (pronounced 'Glahms'). The **Angus Folk Museum** (Easter and May to September, daily from 11am, last tour 4.30pm) is a 19th-century estate of terraced houses. The carefully decorated interiors give an idea of the everyday life of the working population in this period. The contrast between their living conditions and those of the aristocracy will be brought home to you all the more vividly if, after the museum, you pay a visit to ★ **Glamis Castle**, a stately home surrounded by luxuriant gardens (mid-April to mid-October, daily from midday). The seat of the Bowes-Lyon family, where the present Queen Mother spent her youth and Princess Margaret was born, Glamis is opulence itself. The building, which goes back to 1370, was transformed into a splendid manor house in the 17th century. There are said to be more ghosts within its walls than in any other building in Scotland.

Family portraits at Glamis

Montrose is an attractive, friendly place on the North Sea coast with a busy harbour. Its unusual setting on the promontory that separates the Montrose Basin from the sea makes it is a place of pilgrimage for birdwatchers, especially in winter, with huge flocks of wild geese arriving here from the Arctic from November onwards. Skiers on the way to the Cairngorms should make the detour just for the experience of walking on a clear, frosty

Dramatic Dunnottar Castle

day from the Bridge of Dun on the dyke along the river to the point where it flows into the lagoon, with the noise of hundreds of birds coming in to land getting louder by the minute.

Inland from Montrose are two interesting manor houses. The House of Dun (3½ miles/6km west of Montrose) is surrounded by wooded land with marked trails. The house itself is a rather modest but perfect example of the neo-classical architecture created by the Adam family (Easter and end of April to October, daily from 11am). As with all Adams buildings the interior is extremely stylish. **Fasque House** north of Fettercairn (May to September, daily except Friday 1.30–5.30pm) was designed to satisfy all the leisure requirements of upper-class Victorians. In addition to the deer park, the kitchen wing and the servants' quarters are particularly worth seeing. The memorabilia in the elegant rooms of the master and mistress are a must for anyone with an interest in 19th-century history. From 1829 the house was owned by the Gladstone family, whose most famous member lived here when not in his official London residence – William Ewart Gladstone was British Prime Minister no less than four times between 1868 and 1894. In the 19th century he was the most important liberal statesman in Europe and Bismarck's most significant opponent.

Grazing at Fasque House

Nothing could be a greater contrast to Fasque House than ★★ **Dunnottar Castle** on the coast at Stonehaven (April to October, Monday to Saturday from 9am, Sunday from 2pm; November to March, Monday to Friday from 9am). The extensive ruins, with the oldest building dating from the 14th century, are historically important, but it is the unique setting of this castle on top of a sheer cliff which first strikes the visitor. It is deservedly one of the most frequently photographed views in Scotland.

Competing at the Highland Gathering

Stonehaven itself, with its picturesque harbour, is also worth a visit. The Tollbooth Restaurant in its oldest building has excellent fish dishes and vegetarian food.

Further inland we come to the region known as **Royal Deeside,** with the royal residence **Balmoral**. For monarchists and others curious about this aspect of British life, the castle, which was completed in 1855, is accessible on the A93 (ballroom and gardens, May to July, Monday to Saturday from 10am). The royal family regularly spend the latter part of the summer here (when the castle is closed to the public) and unfailingly visit the ★★ **Highland Gathering** in Braemar on the first Saturday in September.

The best adjectives to describe the atmosphere of Banchory are 'solid' and 'respectable'. Solid middle-class antique shops line the main road, and it is not whisky that is distilled here but lavender, in order to make perfume. The distiller is called Ingasetter: it offers tours on weekdays from 9am and also has a shop.

Continue in a northerly direction to **Inverurie.** The small museum in the Town Hall (daily except Wednesday and Sunday from 10am) contains archaeological finds: the surrounding area has numerous prehistoric and ancient sites. On the hill known as **Bennachie** (1,739ft/530m) paths lead up through the woods and moors to the summit with its fine view (accessible on the B9002 northwest of Inverurie). On the nearby summit of **Mither Tap** is a well-preserved Iron-Age fort. There are signposts to sites associated with the Picts and other early settlers on all the roads leading north and west from Inverurie: Brandbutt Stone on the A96, Picardy Stone on the B9002 with Pictish symbols and the **stone circle of Loanhead** on the B9001.

Loanhead stone circle

Cross the attractive green countryside of the old county of Buchan (take secondary roads to appreciate it best) to rejoin the coast at **Fraserburgh**. While the place itself may not seem very inviting, the same can certainly not be said of the 3-mile (5-km) sandy beach in the bay, which is exceptionally clean. The lighthouse of Kinnaird Head was built in 1787 from the tower of the castle which stood on this spot – it is said to be the oldest lighthouse in Scotland. From here follow the north coast via Rosehearty with its attractive campsite by the sea and the imposing ruins of Pitsligo Castle, past the cliffs of Pennan Head and Troup Head and through the rather inconspicuous fishing harbour of Macduff to Banff.

In spite of its many visitors, **Banff** has maintained an aura of unruffled sophistication, to which several buildings by the Adam family have contributed: the simple Town House (town hall, built in 1767) is by John or James Adam and **Banff Palace** is by William Adam, as is the elegant Duff House on the hill south of the centre.

Fraserburgh Sands

Glenfiddich

Those who can tear themselves away from the coast should make for the numerous distilleries on the ★ **Malt Whisky Trail** southwest of Banff. The pagoda-like chimneys of the oast houses around Keith and Dufftown will soon become familiar landmarks, and many distilleries offer tours and a taste of the product – Glenfiddich in Dufftown (November to March, Monday to Friday from 9.30am; April to October daily from 9.30am) and Glenlivet, near the village of the same name (April to October, Monday to Friday from 10am; June to September Monday to Saturday from 10am) cater particularly well for visitors. The best single malt whisky in the region is probably produced by Cragganmore in Ballindalloch on the River Spey (tel: 018072 202 for opening times).

South of Glenlivet in the heart of the **Grampian Mountains** take the time to stop for a while in Tomintoul, one of the highest villages in the Highlands. Take a break from travelling, drink in the scenery and perhaps go for a walk along the river or up into the hills, then drive in a westerly direction to return to the Spey Valley.

Boat of Garten is completely tourist-oriented. Along the two major roads A9/A95 in the valley there is a constant stream of hikers, mountaineers and climbers, mountain bikers and canoeists, anglers and golfers, and, with the first fall of snow, skiers heading for the centres of Aviemore and Cairngorm. At **Loch Garten** nature reserve a round-the-clock watch is kept to ensure the survival of the last ospreys in Scotland. The steam locomotives of the **Strathspey Railway** pull carriages full of tourists through the beautiful countryside between Boat of Garten and Aviemore, and along the 'Ski Road' from Coylumbridge to the Cairngorm lifts is the **Glen More Forest Park**.

Boat of Garten – osprey haven

Strathspey Railway

Cottage at the Battlefield of Culloden

Follow the main road to Inverness a short way and at the village of Daviot take the signposted turning to the ★ **Battlefield of Culloden**. We began this route at the scene of a decisive Scottish victory, and end it at the scene of the crushing defeat which put an end to hopes of Scottish influence in Great Britain. On 16 April 1746 the last battle on British soil was fought here between some 5,000 exhausted Highlanders under the leadership of the Stuart Pretender to the throne, Bonnie Prince Charlie, and 9,000 members of the Duke of Cumberland's elite troops. The Highland Scots were at the end of their strength after the previous campaign and Cumberland was a much more experienced commander.

One thousand two hundred Highlanders are said to have fallen in the battle, and Cumberland acquired the nickname 'the butcher' when he gave orders to massacre all the wounded left on the field plus the onlookers who had come to the scene from Inverness. The visitors' centre is open all year round (April to October from 9am; November to March from 10am), but the best impression of the place is obtained early in the morning on the battlefield itself. When the coloured flags set out at intervals to mark the positions of the troops flutter in the wind against the empty brown moor, the whole tragedy comes eerily to life.

Flora MacDonald in Inverness

Inverness, often called the 'Capital of the Highlands', is by far the largest town in the far north, with a population of 38,000, and is the administrative centre of the huge but thinly-populated Highland Region. It also has the best selection of shops for miles around. The railway lines from Edinburgh and Aberdeen, the line to Kyle of Lochalsh in the east and the only line to the north (Wick/Thurso) all converge at Inverness, and the town is correspondingly busy. Car drivers should note that parking in the centre is difficult and the one-way system confusing.

Mercat Cross, Inverness

Inverness means 'mouth of the Ness'. Follow the river in a southwesterly direction to reach ★★ **Loch Ness**. Although the originator of the most famous photo of the monster recently confessed just before his death that it was a fake, this has not so far done any harm to the tourism generated by 'Nessie'. On the contrary, it is now possible to take an expensive trip by submarine through the loch, which reaches a depth of 984ft (300m). Boat trips on the surface are offered from Inverness, Fort Augustus or Drumnadrochit. In Drumnadrochit there are also two competing monster information centres.

Loch Ness and Urquhart Castle

On the busy A82, after leaving the loch, it is almost impossible to miss the ruins of **Urquhart Castle** (Monday to Saturday from 9.30am, Sunday from 2pm).

Route 6

The Northwest

Ross and Cromarty – Sutherland – Caithness

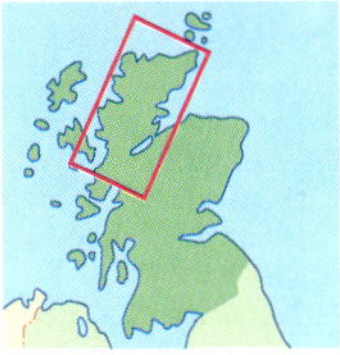

The far northwest of Scotland has no equivalent. No other journey is a preparation for this landscape: soon after leaving Inverness, the distance between the villages and towns increases and once you have reached the rugged Atlantic Coast in the west you will find empty beaches even in the main tourist season. Away from the main road it is sometimes possible to drive for hours without seeing an inhabited house. Fjord-like lochs penetrate deep into the country from the sea and with the numerous freshwater lakes it sometimes seems that the water will soon take over altogether. Every now and then, however, the balance is redressed by a massive rocky peak such as Suilven, which dominates the surrounding landscape. Castles and palaces are rare in the west (with the exception of the odd picturesque ruin), and the region sometimes has the feel of a primitive country still waiting to be discovered. Appearances, however, are deceptive.

Ullapool's famous harbour

The suggested route follows the coast, with a few detours into the interior – and takes you to the end of the mainland in the northeast and to Kyle of Lochalsh, the gateway to Skye, in the southwest. Motorised travellers are at an advantage in this region: trains only go to the east coast, buses primarily serve the main routes, and cyclists must be very fit to tackle the roads here (although they will be greatly rewarded by parts of this route).

This is the place for the holiday of a lifetime – although the tragic history of the region and its pressing environmental problems should never be forgotten.

Dunrobin Castle

ROUTES 6 & 7
THE NORTHWEST
AND HEBRIDES
0
30 miles
0
30 km
N
ATLANTIC
OCEAN
Llunel
Arnol
Shawbost
Uig
Bernera
Stornoway
Portnan
Giuran
Timsgarry
Callanish
7
Outer
Lewis
The Minch
Reiff
Summer
Isles
Achiltibuie
Tarbert
Harris
Hebrides
Leverburgh
Inverewe
Gardens
Gair-
loch
Loch Maree
Kilmuir
Duntulm
Castle
Quirang
Balranald
North
Uist
Lochmaddy
Barpa Langass
Uig
Pobull Fhinn
6
The Little Minch
The Storr
719
Dunvegan
Castle
Dunvegan
Applecross
Benbecula
Portree
Skye
Plockton
Kyle of
Lochalsh
South
Inner
Eilean Donan
Castle
Uist
Lochboisdale
Cuillin Hills
1009
Broadford
Kyleakin
Sea of the
Hebrides
Elgol
Ludag
Hebrides
Clan
Donald
Centre
Barra
Castlebay
Rhum
Point of Sleat
Mallaig
Kisimul
Castle
Oban

Cape Wrath
Durness
Sheigra
Kinloch-
bervie
Handa
Island
Scourie
Tongue
Farr
Bettyhill
Armadale
Dounreay
Thurso
Orkney-
Inseln
Duncansby
Head
Stroma
John
o'Groats
Dunnet
Head
Sinclair
Castle
Girnigoe Castle
Wick
Camster
Latheron
Strathnaver
Kildonan
Loch-
inver
Suilven
731
Ben More
Assynt
998
Loch Shin
Helmsdale
Lairg
Dun Canna
Broch
Ullapool
Dunrobin
Castle
NORTH SEA
Dornoch Castle
Dornoch
Beinn Dearg
1081
NORTHWEST HIGHLANDS
Branderburgh-
Lossiemouth
Elgin
Aberdeen
Dingwall
Nairn
Findhorn
Craigellachie
Inverness
Glass
Loch Ness
Carn Odhar
798
Aviemore
Braemar
GRAMPIAN MOUNTAINS
Pass of
Drumochter
Loch Ericht
Fort
William
Glasgow
Edinburgh
6

The bridge over the **Moray Firth** north of Inverness leads onto the peninsula known as the **Black Isle**, an attractive area with woods in the centre and fine beaches, that is often neglected by travellers speeding past on the A9. The bird sanctuaries of Munlochy Bay and Udale Bay with their many different species of wader are well-known to birdwatchers, and the fishing village of ★ **Cromarty** on the northeastern tip of the peninsula, tidied up for the tourists in recent years, is extremely attractive. In order to include these sights on your tour, take the first turning north on the far side of the bridge – it is not necessary to drive right round the peninsula as there is a car ferry from Cromarty to Nigg on the Fearn Peninsula (half-hourly service between 9am and 6pm). During the ferry ride you may pass an oil rig in tow – it is in Invergordon and the Cromarty Firth area that these monsters are constructed and maintained.

North of the pretty town of Tain the A9 follows the shore of **Dornoch Firth**. To get an idea of what the rural population suffered during the Highland clearances, take the road that leads from Ardgay through Strathcarron Valley to the little church of Croick. In the spring of 1845, a handful of families who had been forced off their rented land in Glencalvie took refuge here and the messages that they scratched in the glass of the church windows, which are still easy to decipher, bear clear testimony to their suffering. Just how densely populated this now deserted area was in those days is indicated by the fact that in 1854 at Wester Gruinards 70 women (whose husbands were either fighting in the Crimean War or had deserted), attempted to resist one of the last clearances in the county and were beaten up by land agents and constables – contemporary reports state that 20 women and girls were seriously injured.

The church at Dornoch

Dornoch on the north shore of the bay is a small, pleasant place, its most important attribute being its main square which has a restored church and the remains of a bishop's palace dating from the 16th century, which today forms part of the pleasant Dornoch Castle Hotel. Golfers will probably think it more important that the famous Royal Dornoch Golf Course lies on the dunes to the south. Golf has been played here since the early 17th century and the present course, designed in 1877 by the legendary Tom Morris senior, is well-known among keen golfers. Nonmembers are also welcome to play here.

From Dornoch, follow the east coast to the north. If withdrawal symptoms set in when the daily itinerary does not include a castle, a quick visit to ★ **Dunrobin Castle** near Golspie is recommended (June to September, Monday to Saturday from 10.30am, Sunday from 1pm; May,

Monday to Thursday 10.30am–12.30pm; gardens open all year round from 9.30am). The seat of the Dukes of Sutherland, who played a leading part in the Highland clearances, it is full of magnificent art objects and furniture. The original building dating from the 13th century was enlarged and transformed into this showy chateau in 1845–50.

The most interesting of the resorts on this coast is ★ **Helmsdale**. The history of the Highlands is presented very clearly at the Timespan Centre (Easter to October, Monday to Saturday from 10am, Sunday from 2pm) with tableaux, sound effects and audio-visual displays. Among the aspects covered are the lives of the Picts and Vikings, the legendary murder in Helmsdale Castle and the clearances in the area. One of the main topics is the gold rush which started at the end of the 19th century when this precious metal was discovered in the Strath of Kildonan. The Tourist Information Centre advertises Goldrush Heritage Tours to the places where it was found. Helmsdale is also the last place that the northbound train follows the coast before turning inland; it then follows a magnificent scenic route and only returns to the coast at Wick or Thurso.

After the village of Lybster watch out for the turn-off to Camster and Watten. This road leads to the **Grey Cairns**, two well-preserved, impressive burial cairns from 2500 BC. They are marked with explanatory signs and it is possible to peer inside. To the southeast, near the coast road, is the **Hill o' Many Stanes**, a complex dating from the early Bronze Age with approximately 200 menhirs arranged in the shape of a fan – it is still not known exactly what their function was.

The part played by Scandinavian invaders and settlers in the history of the far north of Scotland can be seen from the place names alone, which is nowhere more obvious

Helmsdale's fleet

Grey Cairns

Hill o' Many Stanes

Tragic Sinclair and Girnigoe castle

Nesting gulls at Duncansby Head

Spectacular sea-carved cliffs

than in **Wick –** a name derived from the Nordic word *vik* (bay, estuary, trading centre), which is also the stem of Viking. Wick is a busy town with a population of around 8,000 and is equipped to cope with any number of tourists. The Heritage Museum gives a vivid picture of the history of fishing in the region. Looking round the quiet harbour today it is hard to believe the old photos which show it filled with hundreds of fishing boats – more than 1,100 herring boats are said to have been based here in the past.

The lighthouse of **Noss Head** north of Wick is worth a visit. Nearby on the cliffs above Sinclair's Bay are the impressive ruins of **Sinclair and Girnigoe castle**, which has a tragic tale attached to it. In the 16th century the fourth Earl of Sinclair is said to have suspected his son of wanting to murder him and had the young man imprisoned here, where he apparently died in the dungeon seven years later 'lice-ridden and starved'. It is said that the sounds of his wailing and groaning can still be heard in the castle walls. Access to the ruins is rather unsafe and you are advised to take care.

From the harbour of **John o'Groats** there are boat trips to **Orkney**, to the nearby island of **Stroma** and the cliffs of ★ **Duncansby Head**. The trips feature romantic rock formations, seals, huge colonies of birds – and a rough sea, which may spoil the day for some. Although John o'Groats is always known as the northernmost point of the British mainland, Dunnet Head high above the sea, with a view across to Orkney on a clear day, is further north.

Some of the most spectacular scenery in Europe is to be found along the north coast of Scotland. The main road keeps leaving the coast so you must take every minor road to the right if you are not to miss views of lonely bays, rugged cliffs, roaring breakers, seabirds gliding in the wind and distant islands in the mist. On the stretch between John o'Groats and Durness take as a very minimum the turnings to Strathy Point, Armadale, Torrisdale/Skerray and Talmine/Midfield.

One of the most attractive places on this piece of coast is **Thurso**, with good shopping facilities and Scrabster Harbour, where car ferries leave for Stromness on the main Orkney island. One other feature of the area should be mentioned: the atomic power plant **Dounreay** (Thurso owes its well-stocked shops to the custom generated by employees of this establishment). The 'fast breeder' was finally closed down in March 1994 but in 1997 the reprocessing of atomic waste is to be commenced on the same site. The reaction of the local population is mixed: in a thinly populated region with an above-average rate of unemployment more than 850 jobs were lost, which the reprocessing work may replace.

Bettyhill is a pretty village in magnificent surroundings; on the other side of the little bay is the **Invernaver Nature Reserve** with many different species of plants and birds. The **Strath Naver Museum** (May to September, Monday to Saturday from 10am) in a former church gives a good impression of the clearances in the valley south of the village: this detour of around 37 miles (60km) is well worth making if time permits. The road through the historic Strath Naver Valley brings you to a junction at the end of Loch Naver where you will find the Altnaharra Hotel, to be recommended for its superb location and much else besides. From here take either the road north which joins the coast at the charming village of Tongue or the adventurous-looking road northwest which skirts **Ben Hope**, Scotland's northernmost Munro (*see page 90*). It is a long and difficult hike to the top of the 3,041-ft (927-m) summit, and one which should only be undertaken with the proper equipment, but the view is adequate compensation for the effort.

The road follows the shore of the idyllic **Loch Eriboll**, a large bay that stretches back a long way inland, and eventually arrives at **Durness**, which has several rather special features: the impressive **Smoo Cave**, a limestone cave with a high, easily accessible outer chamber; the craft colony of Balnakeil and the famous cliffs of ★★ **Clo Mor** on Cape Wrath. The cape can only be reached by passenger ferry from Keoldale followed by a 30-minute drive in a minibus – exploring on your own is discouraged as the whole area is used by the British army as a shooting range – but the view is wonderful.

For dedicated hikers the most beautiful walk in Scotland is the one from **Cape Wrath** south to **Kinlochbervie**. It should not, however, be undertaken lightly: the 17-mile (28-km) trail is lonely and most of it far from any road, so there is no possibility of breaking off in the middle. However, it does take you along the legendary beach of **Sandwood Bay**, which cannot be reached by car. From the far end of the path, which comes from the south behind Kinlochbervie, it is still nearly 4½ miles (7km) to Sandwood Bay (signposted from Balchrick – reckon on three hours there and back), which ensures that the bay is not overrun with visitors. This is just as well, since this is where mermaids from all around come ashore to rest, a fact reliably confirmed by the local shepherds.

From here the route turns south down the west coast and here the same principle applies as on the north coast: if you stick to the well-made main road and ignore the narrow side roads, you will not discover the real beauty spots of Scotland.

Strath Naver mountainscape

Smoo Cave

Sandwood Bay

Glance from a local

Moody views near Lochinver

Off season in Ullapool

From Tarbet, north of the small resort of Scourie, there are boat trips to the **bird sanctuary** on **Handa Island**. The 15-minute ride (April to September, Monday to Saturday) brings you into close contact with thousands of gulls, guillemots, razorbills, fulmars and cormorants. After the bridge at Kylestrome (until 1984 there was a romantic ferry ride at this point) the B869 turns off to the Point of Stoer and **Lochinver**. Stop for a meal at the Riverside Bistro as you enter the village on the main road – the food is good and they cater for vegetarians.

The best road to take on leaving Lochinver is the one that runs between the coast and the impressive peak known as **Suilven**. This road is described in so many guidebooks as one of the most beautiful on the west Highland coast that it is no longer a well-kept secret and there is more traffic in the main season than the single-track road can really cope with. But this does not make the description any less accurate or the route less attractive. Suilven is climbed every year by numerous mountain hikers; it is not a difficult climb but it is a long one – experienced hikers should allow eight hours there and back from the nearest car park (Glencanisp).

Once on the peninsula of **Coigach,** turn right to get to the beach on Enard Bay near Achnahaird (with an idyllically located campsite). In the southern part of this peninsula is ★ **Achiltibuie**, a long line of houses with a view of the **Summer Isles**. Next to the Summer Isles Hotel is the **Hydroponicum**, often described as the garden of the future (April to October, guided tours at 10am, 12pm, 2pm and 5pm). Here exotic plants are grown in adjustable microclimates and hydrocultures, with solar cells providing the necessary energy.

From Achiltibuie return to the main road to continue towards the south. A turning off the A835 will take you to the **Inverpolly Nature Reserve**, near Knockan, which has an information centre and nature trail (centre May to September, Monday to Saturday from 10am). Continue south to the main centre of the region, **Ullapool**. During the main season the town is often very full, but Ullapool does have a number of attractions, including the campsite on the tongue of land jutting out into **Loch Broom** in the middle of the town. Above this is the charming and slightly eccentric Ceilidh Place, a combination of restaurant and café, hotel and function centre, and on the other shore of Loch Broom is the world-famous Altnaharrie Inn, the only restaurant in the northwest of Scotland with a Michelin star and one of the few that can only be reached by private boat. This fact, combined with the prices, ensures that no-one strays by chance into this exclusive enterprise.

Boat trips to the Summer Isles are strongly recommended (there are several organizers at the harbour), during which, in addition to the superb scenery, you will see cormorants, seals, (with a bit of luck) dolphins and occasionally (with even more luck) a whale. From Ullapool there is also a car ferry to **Stornoway** on the Hebridean Island of **Lewis** (Monday to Saturday three times a day; the crossing takes 3½ hours).

The ferry to Lewis

The fjord-like bays in this area go so far inland that the drive along the coast involves constant detours, but this is more than compensated for by the splendid views along the way. It is easy to be so distracted by all this wonderful scenery that you miss recommended sights such as ★ **Inverewe Gardens** on Loch Ewe north of Poolewe (garden, all year from 9.30am; visitors' centre/souvenir shop April to October, Sunday only in the afternoons; guided tours Easter to October daily 1.30pm). On this piece of land, apparently, nothing was growing but a solitary willow tree when, in 1862, Osgood Mackenzie started to lay out a garden with exotic plants from all over the world. Today the gardens are justifiably the major tourist attraction on this coast, now occupying more than 20 acres (49 hectares) of land, and interlaced with paths which take several hours to explore.

Inspirational gardens at Inverewe

Gairloch has been catering for tourists since the 19th century. The award-winning **Heritage Museum** documents the life of the region's people since the Stone Age and the Mountain Restaurant is a recommended place to eat, especially for vegetarians. Explore some of the minor roads to the beaches and vantage points: the B802 leads north to the appropriately named Big Sands, while the B8056 in the south will take you to Redpoint with a splendid view of the **Isle of Skye**.

Skye and the Cuillins from Kyle of Lochalsh

Loch Maree, southeast of Gairloch, is said to be the most beautiful lake in Scotland. Some might dispute this, but the scenery is certainly outstanding. In Talladale is the Loch Maree Hotel, which is particularly popular with anglers, and at the southern end of this long lake is the visitors' centre of the **Beinn Eighe National Nature Reserve**, which provides information about the flora and fauna of this extensive reserve and is the starting point of two nature trails, both of which lead through the old Caledonian forest.

Applecross

To explore the peninsula of **Applecross** start at Shieldaig, an idyllic place (with its highly commended pub and hotel, Tigh-an-Eilan). The only road takes you along the coast (with wonderful views of the islands of Rona and Raasay). Between the road and the shore there is the occasional ruined cottage – although it is hard to believe, according to parish records there were still almost 2,900 people living here in the first half of the 19th century. In Applecross itself, which consists of two houses, a shop with a café, a public toilet and a campsite, take the narrow road branching off inland which climbs steeply and finally reaches the top of ★★ **Beallach na Bà** pass. The Gaelic name means Cattle Pass, and it was along this magnificent route that cattle were once driven to the market. Today motorists gather here instead to enjoy the splendid view across to the mountains of Skye before embarking on the perilously steep descent into the valley.

The promenade at Plockton

From the south side of the pass **Plockton** can be seen far below on the far side of Loch Carron, but the road winds for miles round the loch before it actually gets there. Plockton's particular attraction is its promenade along the shore against the backdrop of a hillside lined with houses painted in white and pastel colours. The palm trees thrive in the mild climate of the sheltered bay, in which numerous yachts lie at anchor. The Haven Hotel is as charming as the village itself.

Kyle of Lochalsh is still the gateway to the Isle of Skye. The approach to the impressive new toll bridge over the strait of Loch Alsh, which was opened in 1995, bypasses the town, and visitors now drive straight across to Kyleakin on the other side (*see Route 7*).

Eilean Donan Castle

To the east of Kyle of Lochalsch,on the main road through to Fort William (*see Route 8*), is ★ **Eilean Donan Castle**, proudly standing on a rocky peninsula at the confluence of Loch Duich, Loch Alsh and Loch Long. For a long time there was only a ruin here, and it was not until the beginning of the 20th century that restoration was commenced – today it is one of the most photographed subjects in Scotland.

The Black Cuillins of Skye

Route 7

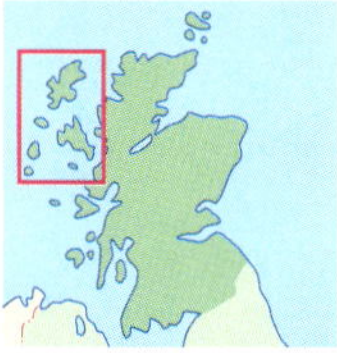

The Hebrides

Skye and the Outer Hebrides

The Outer Hebrides are a holiday destination in themselves, not only for the sea trip, which makes all the islands except of Skye hard to get to, but also because of their individual character. Their landscape and language set them apart from most of the Scottish mainland. Skye is so close to the west coast of Scotland that it is hardly a real island (the new road bridge makes it seem even more like part of the mainland).

The first part of the following route will take you to the dramatic peaks of the Cuillins of Skye and sites connected with the island's varied history. From Uig in the northwest the ferry leaves for Tarbert on Harris. In less than two hours you are in a different world; all the street names are in Gaelic, island life comes to a standstill on Sunday, and the weather is unpredictable even by Scottish standards. The journey then continues by ferry from Harris to North Uist and along the embankments to Benbecula and South Uist. A further short crossing brings you to Barra and from here there is a ferry service to Oban back on the mainland.

Not all the inhabited islands of the Hebrides can be included here, but the suggested route will give you an idea of the largest and most developed of them. Having come once, it is likely that you will be back again for more.

Lost in Skye

As soon as the new bridge from Kyle of Lochalsh to Kyleakin on ★★ **Skye** was completed, the trusty car ferry that had plied its way back and forth for so long went out of service. Kyleakin is where most holidaymakers arrive on the island, but there are other ways of getting there: from Mallaig, south of Skye, there is a car ferry to Armadale seven times a day (crossing time is approximately 30 minutes); this is also the terminus of the railway line from Glasgow/Fort William. There is also a short ferry crossing from Glenelg to Kylerhea and although this can only be reached by single-track road from Shiel Bridge the drive is one of the most beautiful in the area. The Glenelg Inn is a must and the Glenelg Brochs, round stone dwellings from the 1st century AD, are also in the vicinity.

Clan Donald Centre

The southeast of Skye consists of the peninsula of **Sleat** (pronounced Slate), the traditional lands of the MacDonalds. In the **Clan Donald Centre** (April to October, daily from 9.30am) you can learn how the MacDonalds acquired the title 'Lords of the Isles' and became the best organised clan of modern times. Its members come here from all over the world, in particular from North America. North of here, on the coast, if the bank balance permits, you can have a meal cooked for you by the wife of the present clan chief. Together with her husband, Lady Claire MacDonald, who has written several successful Scottish cookery books, runs the exclusive Kinloch Lodge Hotel. To work off the delicious calories, there is a beautiful walk at the southern end of the peninsula (from the chapel in Aird of Sleat, where the road ends, along the path on the other side of the gate to the lighthouse on the Point of Sleat – the journey there and back is around 5½ miles/9km).

The Cuillins are a constant backdrop

The road skirts Bla Bheinn, an impressive mountain with the famous ★★ **Cuillin Hills** as a backdrop, and continues to **Elgol**. At the end of the road, where it drops down to the shore, there is a car park off to the right. Take a deep breath as you get out of your car and give yourself time to absorb the spectacular view. In the foreground to the west is the little island of Soay, since 1953 no longer inhabited all the year round; to the south are the 'Small Isles' of Rhum and Canna and to the northwest are the Cuillins. In the summer there are boat trips from Elgol quay across Loch Scavaig to the mountains opposite, with an opportunity to get out on the opposite shore and climb up to **Loch Coruisk**. Although (or maybe because) it is not easily accessible, this freshwater lake high up in the mountains became one of the most famous views in Scotland, immortalised by romantic painters and poets alike. In his epic poem *The Lord of the Isles* Walter Scott described it as a grim and gloomy place with a total absence of vegetation. This passage was illustrated by William Turner with one of his most dramatic watercolours (*Loch Coruisk, Skye*, National Gallery of Scotland, Edinburgh). However, even these two eminent men should not be taken too literally: the lake is usually bathed in sunshine and surrounded by a proliferation of flowering plants

Mountaineers can take the easy routes up the **Red Cuillins** from Sligachan Hotel on the A850 or venture up the awesome **Black Cuillins** from Glenbrittle: note that this ascent is for experienced climbers only.

On the other side of the Cuillins, follow the A863 along the southwest coast of Skye, with possible detours to the Talisker Whisky Distillery, the Colbost Folk Museum and the Piping Centre in Borreraig, which supplies information on almost everything worth knowing about bagpipes and their music. Eventually, however, the road will bring you to ★ **Dunvegan Castle**, the ancestral seat of the Chief of the MacLeod clan (Easter to October, Monday to Saturday from 10am). Of particular interest are the exhibits from the time of the Jacobite Risings and the clan memorabilia, in particular the 'Fairy Flag'. According to legend the banner was given to the fourth chief by a fairy with whom he had fallen hopelessly in love. It has been unfurled twice to bring the fairy-folk to assist the clan in an emergency – it can only be used once more and then its power will be exhausted.

Dunvegan Castle

The main town on Skye is **Portree**. The picturesque rows of houses on the banks of the loch with shops and bed & breakfast accommodation might tempt you to stay here a little longer. The friendly hotel called Viewfield House, south of the town centre, is equally inviting – unless, that is, you are put off by stuffed animals and dinner round the large family table. Those interested in folk music and dancing should not miss the folk festival at the end of July/beginning of August, and should go to the Gathering Hall on a Friday evening (where joining in the dancing seems to be obligatory).

Picturesque Portree

North of Portree, on the east coast of the peninsula of Trotternish off the A855, are a number of spectacular natural features. The first is the rather bizarre-looking **Old Man of Storr**, highest of a group of rocky pinnacles. It is possible to climb up to it from the car park although the steep paths should be negotiated with some caution and stout shoes are necessary. The view to the south and east is magnificent.

Further north is Loch Mealt, a small lake which sheds its water over the edge of the cliffs into the sea. From the edge of the road Kilt Rock can be seen in the cliffs, with folds and patterns in its strata said to resemble the Scottish national dress. And on the other side of the village of Staffin is a further collection of unusual rocks known as **Quiraing**. In order to examine them close up, turn off at Broraig on the road signposted Uig, which has a car park about 2½ miles (4km) further on. A short but quite strenuous walk will take you to the main group of rock formations with names such as The Needle and The Table.

A hostel for backpackers, a pub with traditional music and dancing and a more sophisticated hotel (Flodigarry Country House) may all be found in close proximity on the A855 north of Quiraing; locals, hotel guests and backpackers all join in the Saturday evening ceilidh in the pub.

Flora MacDonald's house...

...and her grave in Kilmuir

Also in the vicinity is a house once lived in by Flora MacDonald. Her name is associated with the romantic story of Bonnie Prince Charlie, the Young Pretender, who fled to the Hebrides after the crushing defeat of Culloden and was rescued by this courageous young woman. By all accounts Flora MacDonald did risk her life for the prince, although the whole history of the flight, like so much connected with the Jacobite Risings, is characterised by individual heroism, organisational chaos and political naivity in equal measure. Although Flora MacDonald did bring Prince Charlie from the Outer Hebrides to Skye, he thus missed the French ship that arrived at Benbecula three days later to collect him. When the prince finally reached France, John MacDonald of Borodale wrote bitterly: 'And that was how he went away from us, leaving us all in a worse state than he found us'. Flora MacDonald was arrested and imprisoned in the Tower of London; she later went to America but then returned to Skye where she was honoured by her fellow Scots and highly regarded as a conversationalist by such important figures as Samuel Johnson.

Flora MacDonald is buried in **Kilmuir** on the western side of the Trotternish peninsula. The tall Celtic cross in the cemetery above the sea marks the spot where, in 1790, a huge crowd assembled at her funeral. Also in Kilmuir are the thatched cottages of the **Skye Museum of Island Life** (April to October, Monday to Saturday from 9am) which illustrates the lives of the rural population during different eras.

Skye Museum of Island Life

Uig is a small harbour south of Kilmuir, with a car ferry service that runs once or twice a day except on Sunday, and follows a triangular course (the crossing takes 1¾ or 4 hours) between Uig (Skye), Lochmaddy (North Uist) and Tarbert (Harris). This will be a new experience: in the **Outer Hebrides** the local people often speak Gaelic among themselves, and in the schools the children are taught in both English and Gaelic. Church services on both the Protestant islands in the north and the Catholic islands in the south (the religious border runs through the island of Benbecula) are also usually held in Gaelic. On the double island of Lewis and Harris in particular Sunday is still strictly observed as a day of rest – not only are the museums and shops shut, but also most pubs and petrol stations. A leaflet obtainable on the ferry or from the Tourist Information Centre (*see page 97*) will help you read the street names, which are all in Gaelic.

The port of Tarbert

Thus equipped, head along the east coast of the double island (the southern tip is called Hearadh/Harris, the larger northern part Leodhais/Lewis) to Steornabhagh/Stornoway where the information centre will help with accommodation and general information for the whole of the Outer Hebrides. With a population of around 8,100 ★ **Stornoway** is by far the largest place in these islands and thus has the best stocked shops. To learn more about the history of the region visit the **Museum nan Eilean/Western Isles Museum** (June to August, Tuesday to Saturday 10am–12.30pm and 2–5.30pm; September to May, afternoons only) in the Old Town Hall.

Prize catch

From Stornoway cross the moors to the northwest coast on the other side of the island. Here the road divides: turn right to reach the northernmost tip of the island with its lighthouse, Rubha Robhanais/Butt of Lewis. With the sea on all sides there is a real sense of being in the middle of the Atlantic. Return to the road junction and continue southwest, past the **Black House Museum** in **Arnol** (Monday to Saturday from 10am). These 'black houses' were built without chimneys and heated with peat fires, the smoke escaping through the thatched roof.

Beautiful beaches (such as those at Dail Mor/Dalmore and Dail Beag/Dalbeg) are not all the area has to offer; the clatter of weaving looms can be heard from many houses and in Siabost/Shawbost and Carlabhagh/Carloway weavers can be watched at work. The famous **Harris tweed** can only be sold as such if it has been woven on hand-looms on the Outer Hebrides from pure Scottish wool and bears the trade mark of the Harris Tweed Association.

Callanish standing stones

One of the most important prehistoric sites in Europe is to be found at ★★ **Calanais/Callanish**. The stone circle, dominated by a huge menhir, with a burial cairn at the centre and the rows of monoliths pointing outwards from the circle in the rough shape of a cross has been described as 'a crowning achievement of the stone circle architects'. It is situated on a tongue of land jutting out into East Loch Roag, with an uninterrupted view of sea and sky.

At Gearraigh Na H-Aibhe/Garynahine take the B8011 to the south. The scenery, with its moors, rocks, pastures (called 'machair' and typical of these islands) consisting of shell sand with many different kinds of wild flowers growing in it, and endless beaches pounded by the Atlantic, is worth savouring for a little longer. Spend a night at the Baile-Na-Cille hotel at Timsgarry, which is to be recommended for its idyllic location, child-oriented atmosphere and substantial Scottish fare.

Fishing off Harris

To reach the part of the island known as ★★ **Harris**, turn back to the main road. South of Tarbert the beaches on the west coast are even longer and more magnificent. In a climate warm enough for swimming they would be completely full, and there would be dozens of hotels here, of which none would be even half as picturesque or as good as Scarista House on the A895, which is rightly included in most hotel guides.

The ferry from Skye

On the south coast of Harris is **An T-ob/Leverburgh**. The English name of the place is a reference to the large-scale experiment undertaken by the soap magnate Lord Leverhulme (Unilever) in the 1920s. After acquiring the double island in 1918–19 he began to modernise it by building a fishing harbour, buying trawlers and starting to build roads and fish-canneries. On the mainland he opened his own chain of fish shops (called MacFisheries) to sell the catch. He also had plans to rationalize fishing with the latest technology, including the use of planes to search for shoals of herrings. The local population were at first slow to respond to his enthusiasm for development, but were gradually won over by the employment possibilities that were being offered. In 1923 Lord Leverhulme was obliged to let his plans for Lewis drop. Although he continued to invest generously in Harris and Leverburgh, when he died in 1925 his legal heirs stopped all payments. The harbour of Leverburgh however remains as a testimomy to this grandiose project.

For pedestrians and cyclists there is a ferry service from Leverburgh to the small island of Bhearnaraigh/Berneray and Port Nan Long/Newton Ferry on Uibhis A Tuath/North Uist. Motorists must turn back to Tarbert in order to take the car ferry to Loch Na Madadh/Lochmaddy on North Uist. North Uist and the isles to the south, Beinn Na Faoghla/Benbecula and Uibhist A Deas/South Uist, together form a long strip of land connected by embankments. The eastern coastline is rocky, with large bays and small offshore islands, while the western coastline consists primarily of long sandy beaches between promontories. Machair pastures are typical of the interior.

On North Uist the **sanctuary** at **Baile Raghaill/Balranald** is particularly recommended for birdwatchers (those interested should report to the supervisor). It covers an area of 1,626 acres (658 hectares) and has a wide range of habitats: salt water, rocks, sandy beaches, dunes, machair, marsh and freshwater, so it is scarcely surprising that 183 species of bird have been seen here, 50 of which breed in the sanctuary every year.

Also on the island is a well-preserved prehistoric site; the burial cairn of Bharpa Langais/Barpa Langass (on the road from Lochmaddy to Clachan), dates from 1000BC and is said to be the burial place of a person of high standing in the society.

On **Benbecula** it is impossible to ignore the presence of the British Army. Radar stations, a rocket launcher and the barracks in the northwest of the island are not exactly a feast for the eye – but at least the inhabitants have unusually good shopping facilities and an airport which is used by civilian aircraft from Glasgow.

Outside the Pollachar Inn, South Uist

★ **South Uist** is around 20 miles (32 km) long, but only just over 6 miles (10km) across at its widest point. From Loch Baghasdail/Lochboisdale in the southern part of the island, there is a ferry to Barra or Mallaig/Oban on the mainland (Tuesday, Thursday, Friday and Sunday, crossing time to Barra is 1½ hours, to Mallaig/Oban 7–9 hours). The west coast is renowned for its long, sandy beaches, and the eastern part of the island is dominated by the impressive **Ben More** (610m/2,000ft). The views from the summit are quite magnificent. If time and the weather permit, go right to the southern tip of South Uist and sit outside the Pollachar Inn to watch the long drawn-out sunset against a backdrop of islands in the south and the endless Atlantic in the west.

Sand dunes and sandy landing, Barra

★★ **Eilean Bharraigh/Barra** is a particularly charming and friendly place. The main village, Bagh a Chaistail/Castlebay, has a harbour with a castle in the middle of it (Kisimul Castle dating from the 13th century) and there is a lively pub, the Castlebay Bar, near the hotel of the same name. Depending on the season, it may be possible to see the large colony of seals in Seal Bay (information in the Tourist Information Centre).

The famous airstrip on the shell beach of **Traigh Mhor**, which can only be used when the tide is out, is going to be improved (which seems to be a euphemism for concreted over), but until then the flight from Glasgow is will remain one of the most exciting of any made by a scheduled airline.

Inverness
Rhum
Mallaig
Hebrides
Loch nan Uamh
Glenfinnan
Ben Nevis
▲1343
Fort William
Moidart
Castle Tioran
Sanna Bay
Ardnamurchan Point
Strontian
Glencoe
Morvern
Tobermory
Dervaig
Lochaline
Loch Linnhe
Treshnish Isles
Staffa
Craignure
Mull
Duart Castle
Oban
Lochawe
Tyndrum
Kerrera
Kilchurn Castle
Iona
Fionnphort
Loch Awe
Argyll
Firth of Lorn
Inveraray
Auchindrain
Tarbet
Crarae
Loch Fyne
Colonsay
Lochgilphead
Ardlussa
Greenock
Dunoon
Glasgow
Jura
Port Askaig
Tarbert
Rothesay
Kennacraig
Rhinns of Islay
Islay
Claonaig
Port Charlotte
Kintyre
Port Ellen
Portnahaven
Ardrossan
Irvine
Arran
Brodick
Firth of Clyde
N
Machrihanish
Campbeltown
ROUTE 8
THE WEST
0
20 miles
0
20 km
Southend

Route 8

The West

Lochaber – Argyll – The Southern Islands

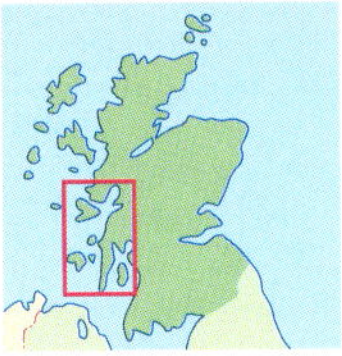

The history of united, Christian Scotland began in the province of Dalriada in what is now Argyll, which was settled by Irish Scots. The Irish monk Columba landed here in the southwest in AD563 and founded the monastery on Iona that became the mother church of Celtic Christianity in Scotland. From Iona, monks were sent to convert the heathens on the mainland. This was the domain of the Scots king Kenneth MacAlpin, who defeated the Picts, joined his kingdom to theirs and gave the Scots their present name.

The long inlets which divide the land up into peninsulas and offshore islands have attracted visitors since prehistoric times, many of whom established themselves in the area. Today, following in the footsteps of the Irish Celts and Vikings, the visitors are tourists making pilgrimages to Iona, sailing on the lochs or attending the Argyllshire Highland Gathering in Oban in August.

The route through Lochaber and Argyll leads first onto the Isle of Mull from Oban and from there north through the beautiful scenery of the peninsulas of Morvern, Ardnamurchan and Moidart to Fort William. It then runs south through Glencoe and follows Loch Awe to the peninsula of Kintyre, with a detour to the islands of Islay and Jura, both famed for their whisky.

The geographical characteristics of this area mean you will spend almost as much time on ferries as on the road, but the views of the countryside from the sea are quite breathtaking.

Man of Iona

The Oban panorama

Oban could be called the gateway to the Hebrides. This is the departure point for the ferries to Mull, Barra, South Uist and Colonsay and the nearby islands of Kerrera and Lismore, and the town is the tourist centre for the whole county of Argyll (today part of the huge region of Strathclyde). Every August the **Argyllshire Highland Gathering** is held in Oban with folk music and traditional dancing. The town is not only a focal point for holidaymakers but also the shopping centre for the rural population of the entire region, so that even outside the main season Oban always seems very busy.

The unusual building, called McCaig's Tower, perched on the hill immediately behind the harbour, may, with a little imagination, remind you of the Colosseum in Rome, at least this was the intention of its designer. The banker John Stuart McCaig, who was a great admirer of Roman art and architecture, had the building erected between 1890 and 1900, partly to provide a source of employment for the local population, but finally he could no longer afford (or was no longer prepared to pay for) the project as costs rose steeply. So the tower was never completed – hence its other name, McCaig's Folly. The view over the loch to Mull and the smaller islands makes the ascent worthwhile.

The best hotel in Oban is on the coast road south of the town centre. Called the Manor House, it has a high reputation, especially for its cuisine.

Castle Stalker off Lismore

Common encounter on Mull

A visit to the island of **Lismore** in **Loch Linnhe** is particularly recommended (a ferry from Oban runs 4–5 times daily except Sunday; approximately 50-minute crossing time; a ferry from Port Appin maintains a continuous service daily until 7pm; approximately 10-minute crossing time, only for pedestrians and cyclists). Points of interest on the island are a round tower (*broch*) dating from the 1st century AD at Tirefour, and the ruins of **Achadun Castle**, a former bishop's palace – the island was the seat of the diocese of Argyll from 1200 to 1507 and the ruins of the former cathedral can also be visited. The first Christian community is said to have been founded here in the 6th century by the Irish St Moluag. According to legend he took part in a race to the island with St Columba: when Columba's boat took the lead near the shore, Moluag is said to have cut off one of his fingers and thrown it on the island in order to claim it for himself.

The other island that can be reached from Oban is ★ **Mull**, after Skye the second most easily accessible Inner Hebridean island (a car ferry to Craignure runs 6–8 times daily, Monday to Saturday, 3–5 times daily on Sunday, and connects with the train to Glasgow; the crossing takes approximately 40 minutes). The ferry passes close to a promontory dominated by the imposing **Duart Castle**. With a few interruptions this castle has been the seat of the chiefs of the MacLean clan since the 14th century, and is worth a visit (May to September, daily from 10.30am). Railway buffs will enjoy a ride on the narrow-gauge line from the pier in Craignure to Torosay Castle, 1½ miles (2½km) away. The castle (Easter to October, daily from 10.30am) was built in 1856 and has attractive gardens. The main town on Mull is ★ **Tobermory**, one of the many settlements which was built more or less overnight in the 18th century by the British Fisheries Society. The brightly-coloured facades of the houses along the shore are a popular subject for photographers and lend the town its cheerful character. Strongarbh House, a Victorian villa on the hill behind the harbour, has a pleasant restaurant and four rooms for overnight guests.

Duart Castle

Tobermory

From Tobermory the single-track B8073 curves round to the southwest, never far away from the coast. After numerous twists and turns with constantly changing views (e.g. of Ben More, the highest mountain on Mull, and the offshore island of Ulva), it joins the road that leads westwards to Fionnphort. From here there is a 5-minute ferry crossing (pedestrians only, no vehicles) to Iona.

Iona Abbey

The island of ★★ **Iona** is the cradle of Scottish Christianity. This is where, in 563, Columba came with his Irish monks to convert the Picts. In subsequent centuries the Vikings invaded the island a number of times, but it was only when Catholic property was expropriated in the 16th century that the monastery ceased to exist. Of the remaining buildings, the **cathedral**, dating from 1500, is by far the largest. Also on the site are the ruins of an early-13th-century convent and smaller chapels. Most of these buildings were in a state of considerable disrepair at the beginning of this century; their restoration was the work of the Iona Community, founded by Dr George Macleod in 1938. The cemetery has great significance for the Scots. Until the 11th century it was the burial place of the Scottish kings, and, in addition to seven Norwegian and four Irish kings, there are said to be 48 Scottish rulers buried here, including Duncan, who was murdered by Macbeth. In Shakespeare's play Rosse asks 'Where is Duncan's body?' and Macduff replies, 'Carried to Colmekill (Icolmkill or Iona); The sacred storehouse of his predecessors/And guardian of their bones'. The cemetery is also the last resting place of John Smith, the much respected politician and leader of Britain's Labour Party from 1992 until his death in 1994.

St Martin's Cross

Iona, or rather the monastery complex, is completely overrun with visitors in the summer. If you can manage it, therefore, it is advisable to take the first morning ferry

Take a boat to Staffa

(usually 8.45am, but check the exact time in advance) or even spend the night here, perhaps in the recommended Argyll Hotel, in order to enjoy the special atmosphere of the place at leisure.

From the quay there are also boat trips to the little island of ★★ **Staffa** with its imposing basalt columns and **Fingal's Cave**, which inspired Mendelssohn to write his *Hebrides Overture* (also called *Fingal's Cave*).

Strontian

From Fishnish in the northeastern part of Mull there is a ferry service to Lochaline on the peninsula of Morvern (Monday to Saturday, every 40 minutes during the day, Sunday every hour; crossing time approximately 15 minutes). From here drive north through the highland valleys of Morvern to Loch Sunart and then west along its northern shore to **Strontian**, the first place of any size along this road. It is not by chance that its name puts one in mind of radioactive isotopes: in the 18th century a new mineral was discovered in the lead mines here which was named strontianite, and the element strontium was isolated from it. The last lead mine was closed at the beginning of the century, but a few new seams have recently been opened and the barite required for the oil drilling in the North Sea is now being mined here.

Still on the shore of Loch Sunart the road now takes you onto the elongated peninsula of **Ardnamurchan**. Those familiar with this part of Scotland will be aware that one of the main attractions of this peninsula – at least for those who could afford it – was the Glenborrodale Castle Hotel, once one of the plushest hotels in Scotland. The impressive Victorian pile has recently been sold, however, and turned into a private home. Sadly it can no longer be visited. Be that as it may, the peninsula still has one particular treat that is worth the long drive to reach it: **Sanna**

Bay. From the car park in Sanna it is possible to walk south along the coast with its sandy beaches and small bays between rocky promontories and dunes to Portuairk. It is just under 2 miles (3km) there and back, and is quite an easy stroll, except that there is no clearly visible path. The numerous stationary caravans that are used by the people of the region as holiday homes do rather spoil the scenery, but they are one way of having a cheap holiday in this area.

To the north of the Ardnamurchan peninsula, the 14th-century ★ **Castle Tioram** is lapped by the tides of the little Loch Moidart. At ebb tide, stranded on the gleaming mud, it looks as if it was washed up there centuries ago, while at high tide it towers majestically out of the water. Its position provides ample explanation why it could never be taken – it was partially destroyed for the first time in only 1715 when the lord of the castle himself set fire to it to prevent it falling into the hands of the Campbells while he and his men were off fighting for the Jacobite cause.

Loch nan Uamh

Loch nan Uamh is also associated with the 18th-century Jacobites; this was where, in July 1745, Bonnie Prince Charlie disembarked from a French brig in order to raise the standard at Glenfinnan. The memorial column (which can be climbed if you are feeling adventurous) at the point where the splendid **Loch Shiel** opens to view, is crowned by the figure of a Highland warrior. It was put up in 1815 by MacDonald of Glenaladale, whose ancestor had marched over the hill with the men of his clan just as the prince feared he had been abandoned by all but a few faithful supporters. The subsequent fate of the region is revealed by the fact that in 1745 the Valley of Glenaladale was able to send 100 men into battle whereas now it is completely uninhabited. In September 1746 a second French ship entered Loch nan Uamh to take a defeated Charles on board and get him out of the country. After this the government troops were once more firmly in charge of the country.

The Glenfinnan memorial

The garrison of the government troops in **Fort William** held out against the rebellions of 1715 and 1745. The fort no longer exists and the town is now exposed to invasions of tourists. The history of the region is well illustrated in the ★ **West Highland Museum** (July and August, Monday to Saturday 9.30am–9pm; June and September, Monday to Saturday 9.30am–5.30pm; October to May, Monday to Saturday 10am–1pm and 2–5pm). Fort William is the regional centre of Lochaber and a key tourist centre: it is the most important stop on the railway line from Glasgow to Mallaig (at certain periods the train is pulled by a steam engine on the beautiful stretch to the west coast); it is the junction of the main roads from the

Ben Nevis

Glorious Glencoe

This way for information

Kilchurn Castle

Grampians, Inverness and the northwest (Skye and Wester Ross), and it is also the starting point of the hike to the top of the highest mountain in Great Britain, **Ben Nevis** (4,406ft/1344m).

The car parks at the foot of wide, well-trodden paths should not deceive you into thinking that this is an easy mountain to climb: it should only be tackled with the proper equipment since it is a hike of 11 miles (18km) there and back and the weather is notoriously unreliable. In the main season the long line of people tramping up may make the expedition seem more like a penance than an adventure, but the view makes an overwhelming impression on everyone who has stood on the summit in fine weather.

South of Fort William on the other side of the bridge at Ballachulish is the village of Glencoe at the entrance to the valley of ★★ **Glencoe**, one of the most impressive, dramatic and romantic places in all of Scotland. The car parks, campsites and visitors' centres, etc. do not detract in the slightest from the overwhelming majesty of the valley. The steeply rising road winds between rock walls that gradually close in until, at the top end of the valley, it comes out onto the open plateau of **Rannoch Moor**. In the valley of Glen Etive mountaineers have been camping out in the wilds for years before embarking on the famous ridge walk over **Aonach Eagach**. This should be attempted only by experienced climbers and is certainly not something for anyone who is afraid of heights.

However, many less adventurous visitors come to the valley to see the location of a notorious episode in Scottish history. In the Visitors' Centre (Easter to October, daily from 10am; June to August from 9.30am) an exhibition which makes the most of modern technology explains how in February 1692 Robert Campbell of Glenlyon arrived with his troops in Glencoe and invented a pretext to ask the resident MacDonalds for accommodation. The government in London had given orders that this powerful, rebellious Highland clan must be taught a lesson, and thus one morning Campbell's soldiers suddenly turned on the valley's inhabitants, killing 38 who were unable to flee with their families into the mountains. The Massacre of Glencoe created a great deal of bad blood between the MacDonalds and Campbells and increased the clans' mistrust of the central government – many Highlanders also interpreted the Jacobite Risings which took place 23 years later as revenge for Glencoe.

After Bridge of Orchy take the B8074 in the direction of Dalmally and Loch Awe. At the north end of **Loch Awe** is the picturesque ruin of ★ **Kilchurn Castle**. To reach Ardanasaig Hotel near **Kilchrenan** for an overnight stay it is necessary to round the end of the loch and drive some distance along single-track roads to the west shore, but the detour is well worthwhile. The manor house, built in 1834, is surrounded by beautiful gardens and not only has extremely attractive rooms but also excellent food.

On the northwest shore of Loch Fyne is **Inverary**. This attractive place, dating from the 18th century, is totally reliant on tourists, who are primarily attracted by the castle. The seat of the Dukes of Argyll and chief of the Campbell clan, it was built at the same time as Inverary itself and has a collection of paintings including works by Gainsborough, Ramsay and Raeburn, and lavishly decorated rooms with porcelain, furniture, tapestries and other treasures (July and August, Monday to Saturday from 10am, Sunday from 1pm; April to June, September and October, closed on Friday).

Inverary Castle

Vernacular style at Auchindrain

Although the **Argyll Wildlife Park** south of Inverary on the A83 (daily from 9.30am) is basically a zoo, it mainly has animals native to Scotland, kept in the most natural surroundings possible. There are sheep and chickens wandering around freely, which are particularly popular with children. **Auchindrain** is a Highland village which has been prevented from falling into ruin and been partially restored to give tourists an idea of life in the Highlands up to the beginning of this century (Easter to September, daily from 10am; April, May, September, closed Saturday). Further south on the shore of the loch is **Crarae Park** (daily from 9am; visitors' centre: Easter to October from 10am). There are three marked paths through the woodlands, with their artifical waterfalls and azaleas, eucalyptus trees and rhododendrons, for which the park is famous. The shortest of these walks takes about 45 minutes.

Whisky in the making

Further along the magnificent loch shore bear south via Lochgilphead and Tarbert/Knapdale to the elongated peninsula of **Kintyre**. From Kennacraig there is a ferry to ★ **Islay** (1–3 times a day; the crossing to Port Ellen takes 2 hours and to Port Askaig 1¾ hours).

The **distilleries** of **Laphroaig** and **Lagavulin** at Port Ellen are open to visitors – the free tastes of these two whiskies are enough by themselves to make the trip to Islay worthwhile. A small turning off on the main road to Bowmore leads to Kintra, which has a beautifully located campsite, a good pub/hotel nearby and 5 miles (8km) of magnificent sandy beach. The golf course on the dunes is said by those in the know to be a particular challenge. There is also a civilian airfield here, but you will seldom be disturbed by it (it is primarily used by golfers making quick trips from Glasgow).

In the west of Islay on the peninsular called the **Rhinns of Islay** is Port Charlotte, a picturesque place where you

Charming Islay

can visit the **Museum of Islay Life**; there is excellent bed and breakfast accommodation to be had in some of the houses along the shore road. Islay has many prehistoric and ancient sites, including the stone circle of Cultoon in the southern part of Rhinns, which it is assumed was never completed. It is thought that the stones lying on the ground did not fall over but were brought to the spot and then never set upright. The island has several well-preserved Celtic crosses, one of which may be found at the church of Kilchoman.

From Port Askaig in the northeast there is a ferry to the island of **Jura** (continuous services during the day except Sunday; the crossing takes 10 minutes): it is the only way to reach this island. The only road here circles the impressive Paps of Jura, with its hunting areas, and winds along the east coast in a northerly direction. This fairly large island (28 miles/45km long and 8 miles/13km across at its widest point) seems to have nobody on it but tourists. In 1947–8 George Orwell came here to work on his novel *1984* and lived at Barnhill, a completely isolated farmhouse in the northern part of the island. The house is not accessible to the public and the walk too strenuous to make it feasible for most people even to go and look at it from the outside. Orwell himself described it as being quite easy to reach, if it were not for the fact that the last 8 miles (13km) had to be covered on foot.

After returning to Kintyre on the mainland, you can either drive south as far as Campbeltown and the **Mull of Kintyre** at the tip of the peninsula, which is only 12½ miles (20km) away from Northern Ireland, or go in an easterly direction straight across the peninsula to Claonaig where there is a ferry to Arran, and finally return to the mainland quite close to Glasgow.

The wild coast of Orkney

Further Attractions

Because this guide is only intended to be brief, certain places every bit as interesting as those described on the previous pages have had to be omitted. Here are just a few of them:

Orkney is a group of approximately 70 islands north of the Scottish mainland (accessible by car ferry from Scrabster/Thurso to Stromness on the main island, Mainland, or by air from Glasgow, Edinburgh, Aberdeen, Inverness and Wick to Kirkwall, also on Mainland).

Orkney is famous for its spectacular setting, but it also has many interesting prehistoric sites: the magnificent Stone-Age grave of Maes Howe and the stone circles of Brodgar and Stenness are all to be found on Mainland, as is the unique Stone-Age settlement of **Skara Brae**.

Shetland is the name of the group of islands even further to the north. Somewhat confusingly, the main island is also called Mainland, with Lerwick its largest town. There are car ferries from Stromness and Aberdeen and in the summer there are shipping connections from Norway and Denmark which also go to Iceland and the Faroes.

Loch Lomond is Scotland's largest lake and one of the country's most popular beauty spots. It runs from north to south, surrounded by picturesque mountain scenery, and has a total length of 23 miles (37km). In the south near the main resorts of Alexandria and Balloch there are so many water sports facilities that the lake has become polluted and overcrowded. Not only is it on the itinerary of the many tourists who visit Scotland, but it is also the destination of thousands of day-trippers from nearby Glasgow.

Guaranteed delivery

The islands of **Arran** and **Bute** in the Firth of Clyde are also extremely popular with Glaswegians. The largest places here (Lochranza and Brodick on Arran, Rothesay on Bute) and the popular beaches become very full during the summer holidays, at weekends and on public holidays, but the beautiful scenery, especially away from the main roads, is more than adequate compensation for the queues at the ferries.

Perth is one of the most important towns in Scotland, and one of the nicest. A pleasant location on the River Tay close to the Highlands, a beautiful old centre, a good selection of cultural events and excellent shops all combine to make it a highly attractive place. It should therefore come as no surprise to learn that in 1990 it was selected as the town with the best quality of life in Great Britain.

MARIA
D G
SCOTIÆ
PIISSIMA REGINA
FRANCIÆ DOTARIA
ANNO
ÆTATIS REGNIQ
36
ANGLICÆ CAPTIVIT
10
S H
1578

Art History

Painting and sculpture

The culture of the Picts has survived solely in the form of metal objects and sculpted stone. The style with which these objects were decorated (with symbols and images of animals) was at first quite distinct from the more ornamental work of the Scots who emigrated from Ireland, but the two styles later blended. Most of the illuminated books and medieval church ornamentation were lost when the monasteries were destroyed in the 16th century – only a few isolated examples remain, which illustrate just how closely the style of the medieval artists in Scotland was connected with that of their counterparts on the European continent. The same is true of court painting, which, until the 17th century, was primarily the province of Flemish and Dutch artists.

An independent Scottish movement developed in the second half of the 16th century, which was reflected in richly decorated room ceilings (Crathes Castle).

With the flowering of the 'Scottish Enlightenment' the 18th century became the era of great portrait painting (Allan Ramsay: *Margaret Lindsay*, Henry Raeburn: *Macdonell of Glengarry*). Both are in the National Gallery of Scotland [NGS], Edinburgh, which provides a good overall survey of Scotland's fine arts. Landscape artists such as Alexander Runciman and Alexander Nasmyth were still wedded to the classical ideal: Greece, Rome and peaceful Lowland landscapes were their subject matter. It was not until the 19th century that the romantic transformation of the Highlands began to be reflected in painting, in, for example, the dramatic genre scenes of David Wilkie (*Distraining for Rent*, NGS) and the lowering landscapes of Horatio McCulloch.

The modern age was heralded by William McTaggert. He began as a genre painter, but his large-scale seascapes, painted at the end of the 19th century (*The Sailing of the Emigrant Ship*, NGS), give an entirely personal impression of the environment. The group of painters known as the Glasgow Boys (including James Guthrie: *A Hind's Daughter*; W.Y. Macgregor: *The Vegetable Stall*; both in the NGS) was strongly influenced by French Impressionism, as was S.J. Peploe who spearheaded the 'colourist' movement at the beginning of the 20th century.

Amongst the artists who are active in Scotland today, John Bellany is particularly well known for his portraits and Ian Hamilton Finlay for his sculptures. The artists who call themselves the Edinburgh Girls (June Redfern, Fionna Carlisle), cultivate an expressive, figurative style; and Ken Currie, born in 1960, has made a name for himself with his dramatic murals for the Glasgow People's Palace.

Opposite: Mary Queen of Scots

Evidence of the Picts near Inverary

'The Painter's Wife' by Ramsay

Drum Castle, Aberdeen

Architecture and design

The fact that a building has been put up in Scotland by no means classifies it as 'Scottish architecture'. In the long history of Scottish architecture not only most of the ideas, but also most of the architects came from the European continent or England. On the other hand, Scotland did produce several architects whose influence spread not only to England, but elsewhere in Europe and beyond.

The beginning of the 14th century saw the development of a specifically Scottish type of fortified complex: the tower house, a massive tower with a kitchen and stables on the ground floor, large hall on the first floor and private apartments above it (Threave Castle, Dumfries and Galloway; Drum Castle, Grampian).

Charlotte Square by the Adam Brothers

Inside Glasgow's City Chambers

In 1700 the splendid age of Scottish neoclassicism was introduced by the architect Colin Campbell, following in the footsteps of Andrea Palladio. The most outstanding representatives of this era were Robert and James Adam, the creators of Charlotte Square in Edinburgh, Hopetoun House and Culzean Castle with its incredible combination of neoclassical elements and romantic castle architecture. The Adams planned every interior down to the tiniest decorative detail.

In the 19th century this kind of elegant simplicity was largely abandoned in favour of the pompous style beloved by Victorian architects, whose monumental buildings with their plethora of ornamentation suitably reflected the commercial pride of their municipal clients (City Chambers, Glasgow). The counter-movement known as the 'Glasgow Style' introduced an independent form of art nouveau architecture: under the leadership of Charles Rennie Mackintosh this group of architects specialised in clear forms and geometric decoration – buildings such as the Glasgow School of Art or Hill House in Helensburgh with their highly unusual combination of tradition and modernity are among the most original in the history of Scottish architecture. Here, too, the interior design of a building was considered to be as important as the exterior.

Literature

Scottish literature has been produced in three different languages. While for a long time only the literature in English was taken seriously, more recently the texts in Scots dialect and Gaelic have been receiving increasing attention. Literature written in the vernacular began to be circulated in 1350 and by 1375 the great Scottish national epic, John Barbour's rhyming chronicle *The Bruce*, had appeared in the English dialect of the Scottish Lowlands. In around 1500 poets such as Robert Henryson and William Dunbar were producing celebrated verse allegories and satires and the cleric Gavin Douglas' rendering of Virgil's *Aeneid* was one of the first versions of classical literature to appear in English.

Rob Roy at the home of Walter Scott

Around 1725, with pastorals such as *The Gentle Shepherd* by Allan Ramsay and James Thomson's *The Seasons* (set to music by Haydn) Scottish literature began to spread throughout Europe. James Macpherson's fabricated 'Transcriptions' of the Ossian poems were published in 1765: the schoolmaster collected Gaelic ballads, which he translated, summarised and published with a faked historical classification as an original Gaelic epic entitled *Fingal*. This sensational 'finding' was the talk of Europe. *Fingal* became the favourite work of many Romantics, who also held the poems of Robert Burns and Walter Scott in high regard. Scott's historical novels (*Waverley, Ivanhoe, Quentin Durward)* were best-sellers in the early 19th century, while Burns' dialect poems earned him the title of 'Scottish national poet'. In the mid-19th century Thomas Carlyle, who had begun his career translating German classic and Romantic writers, contributed significantly to the cultural life of the Victorian age with his historical studies and polemics.

Gaelic literature first became known to a wider public during the Romantic age, when the oral productions of the story-teller Rob Donn MacAoidh (Robert MacKay) and the lyric poet Donnchadh Ban Macan t-Saoir (Duncan Ban Macintyre), whose work is characterised by themes from nature, were written down, translated into English and published. Alasdair Mac Mhaigstir Alasdair (Alexander MacDonald), born in 1695, is considered to be the greatest of the literary Gaelic poets, who followed in the tradition of the old Celtic bards and experimented with their material.

Burns remembered

The 20th century brought a revival of Scottish lyric poetry, both in English (Hugh MacDiarmid: *A Drunk Man*

Looks at the Thistle) and Gaelic (Somhairle MacGill-Eain/Sorley Maclean, born in 1911). And in Scotland there is never a shortage of new talent: in 1994 one of the works most frequently reviewed and highly-praised in the British press was the volume of short stories *Now That You're Back* by the 28-year-old Scots authoress A.L. Kennedy.

Music

To most people the term 'Scottish music' means folk music, or more precisely the bagpipes or the amplified instruments of the folk revival. Even well-informed classical music-lovers would probably be hard put to come up immediately with the name of a Scottish composer. But since the time of the Celtic bards and the medieval Roman-Catholic monks, Scotland has had a tradition of great musicians whose names are now quite unknown: the five masses and two motets composed by the Catholic church musician Robert Carver (born in1485) rank highly, in the opinion of the experts, among contemporary European compositions, although until recently there was no complete edition of Carver's opus. The virtuoso consort music of Tobias Hume (born in 1569) and the airs of John Abell (born in around 1652), who toured France, Italy and Germany as a famous singer, are equally unknown.

Staying in tune

In the 18th and 19th centuries there was a dominant Italian influence in Scottish music, but composers such as James Oswald (born in 1711) also collected folk tunes and preserved them for posterity, while folk music instrumentalists such as the famous fiddler Niel Gow played at the courts of the nobility, where the traditional dances became well-known. These melodies thus found their way to continental Europe and ultimately resurfaced in the 'Scottish' music of Haydn, Beethoven, L.A. Kozeluch, Weber, Mendlessohn-Bartholdy and many others.

Keeping the past alive

The 20th century saw the transition from imitations of European conventional music to modern music acknowledged the world over – from John Blackwood McEwen's impressionistic portrayals of the landscape (*Under Northern Skies*) to the 'dramatic and abstract' forms of Thea Musgrave and the latest international successes of Judith Weir (*A Night at the Chinese Opera*) and James MacMillan.

Scotland's famous folk music has an equally long tradition. Carvings of harps have been found on 8th-century picture stones: as the first national instrument of Scotland the harp was played at the courts of the Picts. Today the Scottish Celtic harp or *clarsach*, a harp without pedals and tuned diatonically, is again becoming increasingly popular.

Harps have a long tradition

Part of the folk revival

The bagpipes, which originally supplanted the harp, were probably introduced from Southern Europe as a pastoral and festive instrument. In around 1600 a complex repertory was developed with a hierarchy of music beginning with the 'small music' (*ceòl beag*), consisting of jigs and reels, etc., followed by the 'middle music' (*ceòl meadhonach*) consisting of slow airs and laments and finally the 'great music' or pibroch (*ceòl mór*), basically variations on a theme, which has been handed down through generations of piping families. The military use of bagpipes with drums dates from the 18th century.

Of the various kinds of bagpipes originally found in Scotland, the Scottish Highland bagpipe is the one most commonly played today, although the Scottish Lowland bagpipe, originally played from about 1750 to 1850, is also heard a great deal; like the Irish Uillean pipes, this instrument is bellows-blown.

The other national instrument of Scotland is the fiddle, which also has a long tradition but became particularly popular in the 18th century; the Shetland Islands have their own repertoire and technique of playing. Latterly the fiddle has been largely displaced by the piano accordion for the accompaniment of dancing.

The modern folk revival involves a mixture of styles. Alongside the pipes, fiddles, flutes and accordions, groups such as Battlefield Band, Capercaillie, Ceolbeg, Tannahill Weavers and Wolfstone also employ rock-music instruments in their repertoires. More traditional forms of music are provided by singers such as Cilla Fisher and Christine Primrose, the harpist Alison Kinnaird, the fiddler Ali Bain or the lowland piper Hamish Moore – to name but a few of the musicians who regularly perform at the countless concerts and festivals that take place up and down the country.

Museum of Island Life, Skye

Museums and Attractions

Unless otherwise stated, all the museums mentioned in the 'Places' section of the guide are open from Monday to Saturday, from 10am at the latest and closing at the earliest at 5pm; on Sundays museums open only in the afternoon, usually from 2pm. Some only open during the summer season, when opening times are in general longer (the Tourist Information Centres provide leaflets containing the exact times).

Edinburgh

Other museums in Edinburgh not mentioned in Route 1 are the ★ **Royal Scottish Museum** in Chambers Street, with craft, natural history and scientific departments in a fine Victorian building, and the ★★ **Scottish National Gallery of Modern Art** in Belford Road, with major 20th-century works by artists such as Picasso, Matisse and Vuillard, German expressionists and Scottish colourists.

Scottish National Gallery

★ **Edinburgh Zoo** (Corstophine Road/A8 west of the city centre, Monday to Saturday from 9am, Sunday from 9.30am) where the animals are successfully kept in natural surroundings (it includes a famous penguin pool). With its child-oriented approach it is extremely popular amongst families, even though keeping animals in zoos has latterly become a problematic issue. Also recommended is the fascinating ★ **Butterfly and Insect World** off the A7 south of the city (bus connection), with hundreds of the most unusual and colourful butterflies from all over the world (1 March to 8 January, summer, 10am–5.30pm, winter, 10am–4.30pm).

Kelvingrove gallery and museum

Glasgow

Other museums not mentioned in Route 2 but worth visiting are the ★ **Museum of Transport** in Argyle Street, opposite the Art Museum in Kelvingrove Park with attractively displayed cars, trams, bicycles, etc. and a whole room full of model ships; the ★ **St Mungo Museum of Religious Life and Art** near the cathedral, which opened, surrounded by controversy, in 1993, is a carefully balanced presentation of the history and practice of the six largest world religions.

Aberdeen

Other museums in the city are the **Cruickshank Botanic Gardens** belonging to the university, opposite St Machar's Cathedral in Old Aberdeen; the ★★ **Satrosphere**, Justice Mill Lane south of Union Street (closed Tuesday), with hands-on science and technology exhibits, a paradise for people of all ages who like pushing buttons, turning handles and generally experimenting.

Edinburgh's Festival Fringe office

Festivals

Edinburgh

Every year for three weeks from the middle of August to the beginning of September Edinburgh explodes into life as it hosts one of the greatest music and theatre festivals in the world, the **International Festival of Music and Drama** (21 Market Street, EH1 1BW, tel: 0131 225 5756, fax: 226 7669). Every concert hall, basement theatre and church hall in the centre of the city overflows with dance groups, theatre companies, string quartets, opera companies and orchestras, and the streets are awash with fire eaters, jugglers, bagpipers, clowns, satirists and theatrical hopefuls of every shape, size and colour. At the same time there are performances by numerous self-financing theatre groups, comedians and mime artists collectively known as the **Festival Fringe** (180 High Street, EH1 1QS, tel: 0131 226 5257), which has now grown so big that it is in danger of outgrowing the city. Also in August are the **International Film Festival** (88 Lothian Road, EH3 9BZ, tel: 0131 228 4051); the **International Jazz Festival** (116 The Canongate, EH8 8DD, tel: 0131 557 1642); and, biannually in 1997, 1999, 2001 etc, the **Book Festival** (137 Dundee Street, EH11 1BG, tel: 0131 228 5444).

Proud to be Scottish

Glasgow

Every year in May Glasgow holds its annual **Mayfest**, an attempt to provide an equivalent to the Edinburgh Festival in attractiveness if not in scope, and it is becoming increasingly popular (18 Albion Street, tel: 0141 552 8000). In June/July every year there are major jazz and folk festivals, and in August **Streetbiz**, a street theatre and entertainment festival (information from the Tourist Information Centre).

Worthington
CAFFREYS
WINES

Food and Drink

Anyone who has ever eaten a traditional Burns' Night supper of haggis, potatoes and mashed swede, could be forgiven for thinking that Scottish cuisine was unimaginative and not very healthy.

This was probably true in Burns' day, but the culinary scene in Scotland is now a lot more varied.

For good cuisine you must of course have good ingredients, and there is certainly no shortage of these in Scotland. The sea, rivers and lochs supply salmon and trout (fish caught in the wild are more expensive but also tastier than those from fish farms) and many other kinds of fish plus mussels, scallops, crabs and lobsters fresh from the cutter. Scotland is rightly famous for its lean beef and lamb – the animals are reared in natural conditions, grazing in the open – and this usually tastes best when prepared simply; venison and game birds are also typical dishes. Potatoes, cabbage, carrots and leeks are the traditional vegetables – and wild mushrooms have now also come into their own. Fruit-growing has a long tradition in the Lowlands, especially the cultivation of berries, and the produce is processed to make desserts and jams.

Oats occupy a special place in the Scottish diet. In 1775 Samuel Johnson famously defined them in his dictionary of the English language as 'a cereal which in England is generally fed to the horses, and in Scotland is eaten by the people'. Oats thrive in colder climates than other cereals, and as a result of the longer ripening process have a higher oil and protein content, so that they are extremely suitable as a basic nutrient for Scottish latitudes. Oatmeal is used to make unsweetened cakes (oatcakes, bannocks), porridge, brose and cloutie dumplings. To make the national dish haggis, oatmeal is added to lamb offal (heart, lights and liver) which is cooked in the lining of a sheep's stomach (it tastes better than it sounds). Coarsely ground oats are also used to make caboc, which is oat-rolled cheese. Visitors who don't fancy the haggis may like to try some atholl brose: thin porridge mixed with honey and whisky.

Honey and whisky are also added to cranachan, which is basically a dessert consisting of toasted oatmeal, fruit and cream. The Scots are known for having a sweet tooth: in the 18th century they were still mainly using honey as a sweetener (and still maintain that their heather honey is the best in the world), but today their sugar consumption is higher than elsewhere in Britain. Their shortbread (shortcake pastry biscuits) is famous all over the world, with its simple recipe known to every schoolchild as 'six, four, two': six parts of flour, four parts of butter and two parts of sugar.

Opposite: Aberdeen's social scene

Try some haggis

Wild salmon is best

A Scottish breakfast may consist not only of the usual egg, bacon and tomato plus toast but also of mushrooms, sausages, smoked fish, porridge, black pudding, fried potatoes and kidneys in brown sauce. This is accompanied by tea, usually made from tea bags (except in the very best hotels or some private homes), or coffee, which the Scots nowadays often prefer to tea, and which can be of very good quality. But strong tea with milk and sugar is still regarded as the universal remedy for any kind of shock.

The Mitre in Edinburgh

Scottish pubs are no longer the exclusively male preserves they used to be. They serve the usual, universally available, soft drinks and local mineral water in addition to various kinds of beer. Warm flat beer is a thing of the past – on the contrary, many of the light lagers with German-sounding names would usually taste better for a little less gas and and a slightly higher temperature. Bitter and stout are obtainable everywhere, and quite a few pubs also offer real ales (e.g. Caledonian, which is primarily obtainable in Edinburgh).

Scotch whisky is exploited for all it is worth by the Scottish tourist trade, and there are numerous distilleries which can be visited (*see Routes 5 and 8*). Scotch is roughly divided into the commoner grain whisky and the expensive, unblended single malt which is produced solely from malted barley and cellared in oak vats for at least eight years. Visitors should try varieties such as Cragganmore or Laphroaig.

Restaurants

The Scottish Tourist Board, and associated tourist organisations, have produced a guide to the country's restaurants, called *Taste of Scotland*. This guide, which appears annually, contains approximately 400 selected and tested eating places with details of location, approach, wheel-

A choice of beers

chair access, smoking restrictions, opening times, specialities (including vegetarian dishes) and accommodation. If you want to be sure of finding well-prepared local cuisine, you may find it very useful (*see Practical Information page 96–7 for tourist office details*). Here we give just a few recommendations for the main cities, as well as the names of some of the best known pubs:

Edinburgh
$$$Merchants Restaurant, 17 Merchant Street, tel: 0131 225 4009 serves innovative and varied French cuisine in smart surroundings. **$$$The Witchery**, Castlehill, tel: 0131 225 5613 is a restaurant with Scottish specialities and atmosphere appropriate to its name, situated directly below the Castle. Edinburgh has a long tradition of good Italian cuisine: one of the best is **$$Tinelli**, 139 Easter Road, tel: 0131 652 1392. **$Henderson's**, 94 Hanover Street, tel: 0131 225 2131 is one of the oldest and most famous vegetarian restaurants in Great Britain. Two of the many pubs particularly recommended are: **The Bow Bar,** Victoria Street/80 West Bow, which has an excellent selection of beers and whiskies; and **Bannerman's**, 212 Cowgate, which has live bands (mostly folk music), a correspondingly lively atmosphere and in addition serves large breakfasts on Sundays from 11am onwards.

Glasgow
The hotel known by its adress, **$$$One Devonshire Gardens**, tel: 0141 339 2001, has a restaurant with an excellent reputation – though its exclusive air may be a little off-putting. **$$$The Ubiquitous Chip,** 12 Ashton Lane /Byres Rd, tel: 0141 334 5007, is a stylish Glasgow institution with fresh fish and an unbeatable wine menu. **$The Granary**, 82 Howard Street, in a quiet location between the new St Enoch shopping centre and the river, is a simple tearoom open until the evening with homemade cakes and vegetarian dishes of the highest quality. Of the numerous pubs only one will be mentioned here, **Blackfriars**, 36 Bell Street, the pub that has everything: live music, stand-up comedians, good food and good beer.

Aberdeen
High quality fish dishes (at correspondingly high prices) can be tried by the harbour at **$$$Silver Darlings,** Pocra Quay/North Pier Road, tel: 01224 576 229. **$The Lemon Tree,** 5 West North Street, tel: 01224 642 230, is a pub and restaurant with a theatre and live music on the first floor. The most famous pub for miles around is **The Prince of Wales** in St Nicholas Lane, which is vast but almost always full and open every day (including Sunday) from 11am to 11pm, with cheap food at midday.

The Ubiquitous Chip

Italian fare in Glasgow

Active Holidays

Cycling can be hard work

Scotland is a country for walkers (and fit, healthy cyclists). The Tourist Information Centres provide maps and descriptions of numerous cycle tours and walks. For a walk in the wind and rain in April or on a light evening after a long sunny day in September it is hard to beat the mile-long, sandy beaches in Wester Ross or the Outer Hebrides, which are often completely deserted.

Hiking

The more energetic can join the 'Munro baggers' – those whose sole aim is to climb all 277 Scottish mountains over 3,000ft (914m). These peaks are named after Sir Hugh Munro who catalogued them in his 30-volume 'Munro Tables' at the end of the 19th century. The fist man to achieve this feat was one Archibald Eneas Robertson, and until the 1970s only around a hundred people had managed to follow all the way in his footsteps. But it has now become a duty for record-hunters (the long-distance runner Mark Elsegood managed all 277 in only 66 days). Normal mortals are advised to take it more slowly.

These mountains are not high by alpine standards, the highest, Ben Nevis, reaching only 4,406 ft (1,344 m). They are nevertheless challenging, bearing in mind that some must be climbed from sea level and that the sudden changes in the weather can endanger even the most experienced of climbers. But this is precisely the attraction of conquering peaks such as An Teallach or Sgurr Alasdair: Munro baggers are not exerting themselves just for the breathtaking view.

Hiking on Ben Nevis

Skiing
The idea of skiing in a romantic landscape has been sold successfully enough to give Scotland a winter tourist season. With five centres, each with 15 to 30 marked slopes and between six and 26 lifts, the central Highlands are the winter sports centre of Britain. Glencoe has interesting runs and a magnificent view, Glenshee and Cairngorm are the largest and most developed areas. Skiing in Scotland does however have certain disadvantages: rapid changes in the weather coming from the Atlantic mean that the snow conditions are not very stable, and on top of this almost impossible to predict. The increasing devastation of the landscape is also cause for great concern: the slopes of Cairn Gorm are being severely eroded, as is all too evident once the snow melts.

Golf
Those whose walking is limited to the golf course will find that golf is a cheap popular sport in Scotland – unless you insist on playing one of the famous courses: St Andrews, Troon or Carnoustie. Golfing enthusiasts should instead try Nairn, Machrihanish or even Royal Dornoch. In the south, in the Lowlands and on the east coast, golf courses are so thick on the ground that being unable to choose between them is the only thing that will stop you from playing. The Scottish Tourist Board's *Scotland Activity Holidays* brochure alone lists 285 places where golf can be played, some of which have several courses (the details provided include addresses, telephone numbers, prices, admission restrictions, etc).

A golfing mecca

Surfing
Surfing and windsurfing are becoming increasingly popular, which is scarcely surprising given Scotland's superb beaches, and good instruction for beginners is often available. For information contact the Scottish Windsurfing Association, c/o RYA Scotland, Caledonia House, South Gyle, Edinburgh, tel. 0131 317 7217. For seasoned surfers, the Hebridean island of Tiree west of Mull, though not very easy to get to, has the most hours of sun in Scotland and extremely demanding wind conditions.

Sailing
In Scotland there is a more unusual way of exploring the country – by sea. Boat trips through the magnificent island world off the west coast are always to be recommended, but those who want to take the helm themselves should request information about boat hire, sailing courses, legal requirements, etc. from the Royal Yachting Association Scotland, Caledonia House, South Gyle, Edinburgh, tel. 0131 317 7388.

Outward bound off Thurso

828

Getting There

Opposite: All aboard the Strathspey

By air

British Airways flies every hour from Heathrow to both Edinburgh and Glasgow and there are also regular British Airways flights from Manchester and Birmingham. From Heathrow and several English regional airports, Edinburgh and Glasgow are also served by British Midland and Air UK; Aberdeen is served by Brit Air and Air UK and Inverness is served by British Airways.

Most transatlantic flights to Scotland use Glasgow airport: both American Airlines and British Airways have regular flights and a number of charter companies fly from the United States and Canada. In summer there is one transatlantic flight a week from JFK airport to Edinburgh.

Edinburgh airport (tel: 0131 333 1000) is 6 miles (10km) west of the city centre with good road access and a useful airlink bus service to the heart of town. Glasgow airport (tel: 0141 887 1111) is 8 miles (13km) west of the city centre alongside the A8 motorway at junction 28. A coach service runs between the airport and Anderston and Buchanan bus stations in the heart of the city.

In Scotland, BA Express, otherwise known as Loganair, operates regular services between Glasgow and the Western Isles (Benbecula, Barra and Lewis); it is also possible to fly to Benbecula and Lewis from Inverness.

By rail

There is a regular train service from London. For details contact British Rail, tel: 0171 387 7070 (for journeys via the west coast); or tel: 0171 278 2477 (for journeys via the east coast)

Glasgow Central Station

By bus

The cheapest form of public transport to Scotland is the long-distance bus, using the National Express service from England or Scottish Citylink (which, for example, runs buses three to five times daily from London to Edinburgh or Glasgow, a journey of 8–9 hours).
National Express: for journeys to Edinburgh, tel; 0171 617 8089; for journeys to Glasgow, tel: 0171 617 8083.
Scottish Citylink: tel: 0141 332 9191.

By car

Scotland is easily reached by car from major centres in England. From London, travellers can take the M40 motorway to Birmingham, the M6 to Carlisle and then on to Glasgow and destinations in the west of Scotland. For Edinburgh and the east, the A1, which is partly motorway, is the fastest route north, crossing the border near Berwick-upon-Tweed.

Getting Around

By road

Options on Skye

The most important thing for visitors from outside Britain to remember when travelling in Scotland or the rest of the United Kingdom, is that the British drive on the left.

Speed limits are 30 mph (48 km/h) in built-up areas, 60 mph (96 km/h) on ordinary roads and 70 mph miles (113 km/h) on motorways or dual carriageways. There are a few other points to note. Traffic already on a roundabout has right of way (and there are many junctions with roundabouts). The many single-lane roads with passing places, especially in the Highlands, are a delight, although their use requires a certain amount of caution (let the locals overtake). Stray sheep tend to cross the road just when one of the few cars you will meet on your journey is passing. But that is the only real hazard – Scotland's roads are relatively safe.

Hire cars are not cheap, but can be obtained at airports and in the larger towns from the usual companies. The requirements are a minimum age of 21, a driving licence and, preferably, a credit card.

Hertz: in Edinburgh: tel: 0131 556 8311; Edinburgh airport: tel: 0131 333 1019; in Glasgow: tel: 0141 248 7736; Glasgow airport: 0141 887 2451.

Avis: in Edinburgh: tel: 0131 337 6363; Edinburgh airport: tel: 0131 333 1866.; Glasgow: tel: 0141 221 2827; Glasgow airport: 0141 887 2261.

Both the Automobile Association (AA) and the Royal Automobile Club (RAC) have reciprocal arrangements with North American motoring associations. For emergency assistance there are clearly marked telephones at the roadside and members who need help should have the name of

Speeding through Glencoe

their organisation and their membership number ready when they ring.

By rail

Scotland has some spectacular railway routes (e.g. the West Highland Line from Glasgow via Fort William to Mallaig), but only one that goes to the far north: from Inverness, branching off after Halkirk to Wick or Thurso.

By bus

Bus connections in country areas have been severely 'thinned out' – some places can only be reached by bus once a day, and not at all on Sunday and public holidays. Bus services within the larger cities, however, are usually quite efficient.

By bike

Cyclists do not have an easy time of it in Scotland because there are so many hills, but there are other compensations. Away from the main highways there are numerous narrow roads with surprisingly good surfaces. Apart from the occasional local driver on urgent business or the milk tankers that hurtle from farm to farm, you will frequently have these roads to yourself.

Information about the hire of bicycles, train connections within Scotland and ferries and flights to the islands, etc. can be obtained from the central information service of the Scottish Tourist Board, tel: 0131 332 2433.

City transport

Bus is the main form of transport in Edinburgh. In Glasgow there is an underground railway, which runs round the periphery of the city centre, as well as orange city buses. A special bus line connects Glasgow's two main stations, Central Station (for England and the Southeast/shuttle to the ferry to Ireland in Stranraer) and Queen Street Station (the North/the Highlands, the East/Edinburgh). More detailed information can be obtained from the St Enoch Square Travel Centre.

By Ferry

Caledonian MacBrayne has a near monopoly on west coast routes. Its 30 vessels call at 53 ports on the mainland and serve 23 islands. They sell hopscotch tickets and, best value for visitors with cars, rover tickets for driver and one passenger giving 8 or 15 days unlimited travel on most routes. Boats vary from the large, well-equipped car ferries operating to the Outer Hebrides to smaller vessels with wooden seats and minimal refreshments. For further information, contact: Caledonian MacBrayne, Ferry Terminal, Gourock, PA19 1QP, tel: 01475 650102.

Island ferry

Facts for the Visitor

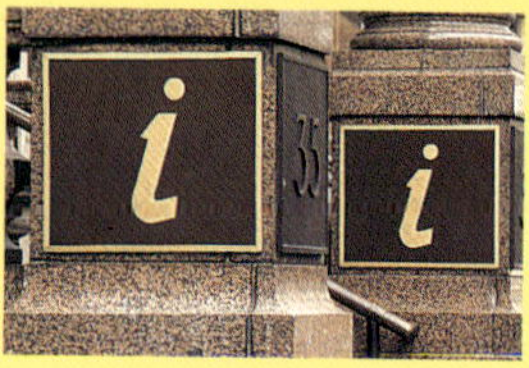

Travel documents

The same entry regulations apply as in the rest of the United Kingdom. Visitors from North America, Japan, most former Commonwealth countries and EU countries do not need a visa for short stays. Check with the British Embassy in your home country if in doubt.

Tourist information

For visitors from North America, information about Scotland ia available through the **British Tourist Authority**.
In Canada
94 Cumberland Street, Suite 600, Toronto, Ontario M5R 3N3, tel: (416) 961 8124.
In the US
John Hancock Centre, Suite 2230, 875 N Michigan Avenue, Chicago, Illinois, 60611, tel: (312) 787 0490; Plaza of the Americas, North Tower, Suite 750. Lock Box 346, Dallas, Texas 75201, tel: (214) 720 4040; 612 South Flower Street, Los Angeles, California 90017, tel: (213) 623 8196; 3rd Floor, 40 West 57th Steet, New York, NY 10019, tel: (212) 581 4708.

In the UK visitors can write to the **Scottish Tourist Board** at 23 Ravelston Terrace, Edinburgh, EH4 3EU, tel: (0131) 557 1700; the Scottish Tourist Board also runs an information centre at 9 Cockspur Street, London SW14 5BL, tel: 0171 930 8661.
In addition to the above, Scotland's local tourist boards have their own information centres (TICs):

Edinburgh
Tourist Information Centre (TIC), 3 Princes Street, Edinburgh EH2 2QP (Waverley Market, at the main station), tel: 0131 557 1700, fax: 557 5118.

Glasgow
Tourist Information Centre (TIC), 39 St Vincent Place, Glasgow G1 2ER (between George Square and Buchanan Street), tel: 0141 204 4400, fax: 204 4772.

Aberdeen
Tourist Information Centre (TIC), St Nicholas House, Broad Street, Aberdeen AB19 1DE (opposite Marischal College), tel: 01224 632 727, fax: 620 415. Can provide information about the Aberdeen Highland Games in June and the numerous other Highland Games held in the area, including the Braemar Highland Gathering, and about the Scottish Connection Festival, a festival of Scottish culture held every Easter.

Glasgow shoppers

TICs in other parts of the country are as follows:

Ayr, tel: 01292 288688; Castlebay, tel: 01871 810 336 (summer only); Dornoch, tel: 01862 810 400; Dumfries, tel: 01387 253862; Dundee, tel: 01382 434664; Durness, tel: 01971 511259 (summer only); Fort William, tel: 01397 703781; Gairloch, tel: 01445 712 130; Helmsdale, tel: 01431 821640 (summer only); Inverary, tel: 01499 302063; Inverness, tel: 01463 234 353; fax: 710 609; Inverurie, tel: 01467 620600; Kyle of Lochalsh, tel: 01599 534276; Lochinver, tel: 01571 844330; Montrose, tel: 01674 672000; Oban, tel: 01631 563122; Peebles, tel: 01721 720138; Portree, tel: 01478 612137; St Andrews, tel: 01334 472021; Stirling, tel: 01786 475019; Stornoway, tel: 01851 703088; Tarbert (Harris), tel: 01859 502011 (summer only); Thurso, tel: 01847 892371 (summer only); Tobermory, tel: 01688 302182; Ullapool, tel: 01854 612135 (summer only); Wick, tel: 01955 602596.

Currency

The monetary unit is the pound sterling, as in the rest of Great Britain: £1 = 100 pence. In addition to the Bank of England notes and coins, notes issued by the Bank of Scotland and Royal Bank of Scotland are also in circulation (same value and size, different designs), in denominations of £1, £5, £10, £20, £50 and £100 notes, and 1, 2, 5, 10, 20, 50 pence and £1 coins. Scottish bank notes are legal tender throughout Britain, but you may have difficulty changing them elsewhere.

The usual credit cards are taken by most hotels, restaurants, shops and petrol stations, etc. (the relevant signs are displayed on the doors).

The Royal Bank of Scotland

Tipping

Taxi drivers expect about 10–15 percent of the fare. Waiters in restaurants should also be given 10–15 percent of the bill, if it is stated on the menu that service is not included (otherwise it is left to the discretion of the customer to show appreciation of good service). Bar staff in pubs etc. are not usually tipped. Tip porters and page boys 50p upwards. For good service in a country house hotel, leave something for the staff when you pay at reception. Scotland is not in general a country where a lot of tipping is expected.

Opening times

Shops

As in the rest of Britain, most shops open from 9.00am–5.30pm. Supermarkets often stay open much later. Some shops, particularly in smaller towns and villages, close on Saturday afternoon, and some have a mid-week half-day closure. The main difference in Scotland is that you are less likely to find shops open on Sunday, especially in the rural areas.

Banks

Monday to Friday 9.30am–12.30pm and 1.30–3.30pm. Some in the larger cities are open longer

Unexpected purchases

Shopping and souvenirs

Edinburgh

Exclusive and unusual shops are to be found in the area between Princes Street and George Street; on Princes Street you will find not only numerous tartan, tweed and wool shops, but also **Jenners**, generally known as the 'Harrods of Edinburgh'; gift articles, souvenirs and 'Scottish specialities' are available in abundance along the Royal Mile, while in and around St Stephen Street and North West Circus Place there is a concentration of antique and second-hand shops.

Glasgow

Glasgow's markets are justifiably famous and not to be missed. Try the **Fishmarket** in Clyde street, the weekend **Fruitmarket** in Candleriggs to the north and the famous **Barrows** fleamarket in Gallowgate to the east.

For more local colour there is **Paddy's Market** situated in the lanes between Clyde Street and Bridgegate. **Argyll Street**, **Sauchiehall Street** and the more upmarket **Buchanan Street** are Glasgow's great shopping thoroughfares. They are supplemented by a number of new shopping malls, including the impressive **Princes Square** just off Buchanan Street.

Aberdeen

Everything you need (and much that you do not) can be found in the **Bon Accord Centre** and **St Nicholas Centre** in the inner city; in George Street north of the Bon Accord Centre there are some interesting second-hand and antique shops.

Public holidays
New Year's Day, Good Friday, the first Monday in May, the last Monday in May, the first Monday in August, and 25 and 26 December.

Postal services
Post offices are usually open from Monday to Friday from 9am to 5.30pm, Saturday often only till 1pm. The sub-post offices, i.e. postal counters in village shops, usually close at midday and/or one afternoon in the week.

Remote mail

Telephones
The famous red telephone boxes have largely disappeared. Modern telephones accept 5, 10, 20 and 50 pence pieces, also pound coins, and the minimum amount is 10p. There are card phones almost everywhere: cards ranging from £1 to £20 are obtainable from newsagents and tobacconists, etc. displaying the green and white Phonecard sign. Long distance and international calls can be made from all public telephone boxes, with cheap rates from 6pm to 8am on weekdays and all day on Sunday and public holidays. To call the US and Canada, dial 001 followed by the code and number. National inquiries tel: 192, international inquiries tel: 153.

Disabled travellers
The Scottish Council on Disability (Disability Scotland) will answer all relevant inquiries. A detailed list of hotels/bed and breakfasts, camp sites, sports centres, etc. with facilities for the disabled may be obtained from Disability Scotland, Princes House, 5 Shandwick Place, Edinburgh EH2 4RG, tel: 0131 229 8632, fax: 229 5168.

Newspapers
The Scotsman and the Sunday paper *Scotland on Sunday* are recommended for detailed reports on Scottish affairs as well as international news (the latter also has good restaurant tips and travel and culture articles). Scotland also has the popular newpapers *Daily Record*, *Sunday Post* and *Sunday Mail*, and in most parts of the country all the English daily papers are available.

Radio and television
Four television channels broadcast throughout the country: BBC1, BBC2, ITV (or the associated regional channels) and Channel 4. Details of the programmes are given in the daily press and in a number of broadcasting magazines, of which Radio Times and TV Times are the most widely circulated. The BBC has five national radio stations, and there are also regional BBC stations and numerous commercial radio stations.

Dressed for the occasion

Clothing

You should take waterproofs and warm clothing whenever you go to Scotland. It is not necessary to dress up for concerts or the theatre, but some more expensive restaurants expect men to wear jackets and ties and women skirts or dresses for dinner.

Time

In winter Great Britain is on Greenwich Mean Time (GMT), one hour earlier than Central European Time. In March the country goes onto summer time, when the clocks are put forward one hour; at the end of October they are put back an hour.

Electricity

Electricity is 240V/50 Hz AC. Equipment designed for 220V AC can be used with an adapter.

Health care

Visitors from other parts of Britain are entitled to free treatment under the National Health Service. For visitors from abroad, emergency treatment is free under the National Health Service, but other treatment must be paid for. Citizens of EU countries benefit from a reciprocal health-care agreement with Britain. However, it is always wise to have good private health insurance cover. National Health Service prescription charges are high – approximately £5 per item – and many medicines are cheaper when bought over the counter from a chemist.

Emergencies

The emergency number throughout Britain is 999. When you dial it (the calls are free) you will be asked whether you want the police, fire service or ambulance, and possibly also the coastguard or mountain rescue service. Have the number that you are calling from ready, and the address or location where help is needed.

Further learning

For those interested in learning more about Scottish culture there are Gaelic courses and instruction in every kind of traditional craft in the Sabhal Mor Ostaig Gaelic School, An Teanga, Isle of Skye, tel. 014714 844373.

Diplomatic representation

American Consulate General: 3 Regent Terrace, Edinburgh EH7, tel: 0131 556 8315.

Australian High Commission: Australia House, Strand, London WC2B 4LA, tel: 0171 438 8535.

Canadian High Commission: Macdonald House, 1 Grosvenor Square, London W1, tel: 0171 258 6600

Accommodation

Scotland is made for the independent traveller, with lodgings from the prohibitively expensive to simple bed & breakfast accommodation, camp sites and youth hostels. Scotland is well provided with camp sites, especially on the southern coasts and of course at all the tourist spots, but there are two problems with camping in Scotland: the weather and the midges. Holiday cottages and flats are also a popular alternative for all those who have decided beforehand where they want to spend their holiday.

A complete list of Scottish TICs and brochures on all types of accommodation can be obtained from the central information service of the Scottish Tourist Board, tel: 0131 334 2433). The Scottish Youth Hostel Association (7 Glebe Crescent, Stirling FK8 2JA, tel: 01786 451181) also publishes a list of its hostels.

Cheap accommodation, which is available to everyone, not just to students, is provided by the universities of Edinburgh, Glasgow, Dundee, St Andrews, Stirling and Strathclyde. For information contact the BUAC (British Universities Accommodation Consortium Limited), Box H9 University Park, Nottingham, NG7 2RD.

Outside the busy summer season it is quite possible to explore Scotland without planning everything in advance. Here it cannot be said often enough how helpful the Tourist Information Centres are.
Here are a few recommendations:

Edinburgh
$$$The Caledonian, Princes Street, EH1 2AB, tel: 0131 225 2433, fax 225 6632 is a luxury city hotel, excellently located. **$$Sibbet House** 26/28 Northumberland Street, EH3 6LS, tel: 0131 557 8036, fax 558 3453, created from two elegant residences in the New Town, is reasonably priced for what it offers, but has become very popular and is often booked out. The 'official' hostel of the **$YHA**, 18 Eglinton Crescent, tel: 0131 337 1120 is not only friendly, but also a magnificent piece of architecture. **$$$Borthwick Castle**, tel: 01875 820514 is a real castle with every comfort (at a price) within reasonable distance of the city (16 miles/26 km) from the centre in North Middleton south of Dalkeith.

Glasgow
The hotel known by its address as **$$$One Devonshire Gardens**, Glasgow G12 OUX, tel: 0141 339 2001, fax: 337 1663 is a very smart hotel with an equally smart restaurant. **Babbity Bowster**, 16 Blackfriars Street, G1 1PE, tel: 0141 552 5055 is a small centrally located hotel with a lively pub, appropriately named after a Scottish folk dance.

Campers

Edinburgh Youth Hostel

Loch Torridon Hotel at Inverewe

A cheap place to stay, during the university holidays is **$Baird Hall,** Strathclyde University, 460 Sauchiehall Street, tel: 0141 332 6415, which has splendid art deco embellishments. **$$$Gleddoch House,** Langbank, tel: 01475 540711, fax: 540201 is a luxurious country house with excellent Scottish cuisine and a golf course, only 48 miles (30 km) from the city centre, with good road connections.

Aberdeen
$$$The Caledonian Thistle,** 10–14 Union Terrace, AB9 1HE, tel: 01224 640233, fax 641627, is a traditional city hotel. The **$$Craiglynn Hotel, 36 Fonthill Road, AB1 2UJ, tel/fax: 01224 584050 offers Victorian elegance and Scottish cuisine at reasonable prices.

Aviemore
$$$Cairngorms Hotel, tel: 01479 810233, fax: 810791. Elegant luxury.

Cairngorms Hotel

Auchencairn
$$$Balcary Bay Hotel, tel: 01556 640217, fax: 640272. Overlooking the bay. Delicious food. Expensive.

Ayr
$$Burns Monument Hotel, Alloway, tel: 01292 442466, fax: 443 174. Pleasant and reasonable. **$$Northpark House**, near Belleisle Golf Course, tel: 01292 442336.

Banchory (near Balmoral)
$$$Banchory Lodge, tel: 01330 22625, fax: 5019. Expensive. **$$$Raemoir House**, tel: 01330 24884, fax: 2171. Expensive. **$$$Invery House,** tel: 01330 24782, fax: 4712. The most expensive and luxurious of the three Balmoral hotels, with its own forest and fishing runs

Bettyhill
$$Altnaharra Hotel, tel and fax: 0154 41 222. Superb location near Loch Naver.

Dornoch
$$$Dornoch Castle, tel: 01862 810216, fax: 810981. Near Royal Dornoch Golf Course.

Fort William
$$$Inverlochy Castle Hotel, tel: 01397 702177, fax: 702953. Luxurious splendour.

Harris
$$$Scarista House, on A895, tel: 01859 550238, fax: 550277. Picturesque and highly recommended.

Inverness
$$$Dunain Park Hotel, tel: 01463 230512, fax: 224532. Sauna and swimming pool.

Kelso
$$$Sunlaws House, on the A698 3 miles (5 km) south of Kelso, tel: 01573 450331, fax: 450611. Excellent food and accommodation in this Victorian manor.

Kilchrenan (Loch Awe)
$$$Ardanasaig Hotel, tel: 018663 333, fax: 222. Old manor house on the lake, with beautiful grounds and excellent food.

Ardanasaig Hotel

Lochinver
$$Albannach Hotel, tel and fax: 01571 844407. Good food and accommodation in Baddidarach, 2km from Lochinver.

Peebles
$$Peebles Hydro, Innerleithern Road, tel: 01721 720602, fax: 722999. Famous spa hotel.

Selkirk
$$$Philipburn House Hotel, junction of A707 and A798, tel: 01750 20747, fax: 21690. Hotel caters particularly well to vegetarians and children.

Skye
$$$Kinloch Lodge Hotel, Sleat, tel: 01471 833214, fax: 833277. Wonderful restaurant. **$$Viewfield House**, Portree, tel: 01478 612217, fax: 613517. Family-run hotel. **$$Flodigarry Country House**, Quiraing, tel: 01470 552203, fax: 552301. On the A855 north of the cliffs.

Flodigarry Country House on Skye

St Andrews
$$$Old Course Hotel, tel: 013344 74371, fax: 77668. **$$$Peat Inn**, southwest of town, tel: 01334 840206.

Stirling
$$$Park Lodge Hotel, 32 Park Terrace, tel: 01786 474862, fax: 449748. Elegant accomodation.

Talladale
$$Loch Maree Hotel, tel: 01445 760288. Near one of the most beautiful lochs in Scotland.

Ullapool
$$Ceilidh Place, West Argyle Street, tel: 01854 612103. Eccentric but charming. **$$$Altnaharrie Inn,** shores of Loch Broom, tel: 01854 633230. Accessible only by boat.

Index